CLASSICAL STUDIES for TENOR BANJO

Rob MacKillop

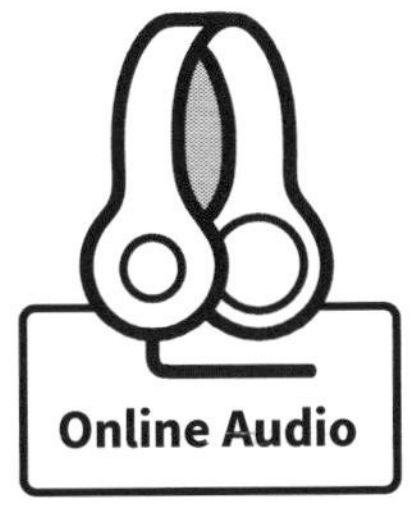

To access the online audio go to:
WWW.MELBAY.COM/30993MEB

The Deering Sierra 19-Fret Tenor Banjo with Fiberskyn Head on the cover is courtesy of Deering Banjo Company.

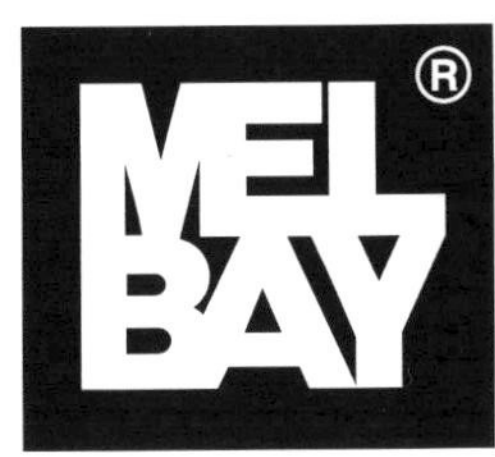

WWW.MELBAY.COM

Contents

About the Author

"One of Scotland's finest musicians" Celtic World
"A top-drawer player" Early Music Today
"MacKillop displays dazzling virtuosity...the playing is exceptionally musical." Sounding Strings

Rob MacKillop has recorded multiple CDs of historical music, three of which reached the number one position in the Scottish Classical Music Chart. In 2001 he was awarded a Churchill Fellowship for his research into medieval Scottish music, which led him to study with Sufi musicians in Istanbul and Morocco. He broadcast an entire solo concert on BBC Radio 3 from John Smith's Square, London. He has presented academic papers at conferences in Portugal and Germany and has been published many times. Rob has been active in both historical and contemporary music.

An experienced teacher (Royal Scottish Academy of Music, Napier University Edinburgh, etc) Rob now teaches people around the world via Zoom from his home studio in Edinburgh. Contact can be made via his website, http://RobMacKillop.net

INTRODUCTION

The tenor banjo slowly morphed into existence in the first fifteen or so years of the 20th century. Mandolin players, who were used to playing melodic lines in 5ths tuning in classical fretted orchestras and smaller ensembles, were in demand as a new dance craze took hold. But for dance bands a louder instrument was required. Early attempts at a mandolin-banjo (more of the former than the latter) were doomed to relative failure, and were soon replaced by banjo-mandolins (more of the former than the latter) with four single strings. A brief tribal tuning war eventually settled in favor of CGDA; the same tuning as the mandola and viola.

The new tenor banjo was well placed to embrace the new tango revolution, and early advertisements referred to it as the *tango banjo*, which however proved to be a short-lived name. Soon the jazz craze took off, and the tenor banjo in CGDA tuning found itself the most in-demand accompaniment instrument, no longer playing melodies but strumming rhythmical chords.

The melodic style is evident in that other popular tenor-banjo development: Irish traditional music. Here the banjo is mostly tuned like a violin, GDAE, although some players still use the CGDA tuning.

As much as I love jazz and traditional Irish music, it has long been my view that the tenor banjo has much to offer in the classical music realm; indeed, many of the early tenor-banjo method books contain classical works by, among others: Offenbach, Donizetti, Grieg, Mozart, Verdi, Puccini, and even Wagner.

More recently, tenor banjoists have explored baroque music (see my *Bach's Cello Suites I-III Arranged for Tenor Banjo*, Mel Bay 30430M) and other historical styles, both as soloists and in ensembles. However, Bach's music is advanced, and I have felt the need to compile a book of studies and pieces from classical method books to help prepare the modern player for the finest classical repertoire.

To do so, I have drawn together excellent technical and musical studies from method books for the mandolin (which has a very long classical music history) and cello, as well as guitar.

The cello has the same number of strings as the tenor banjo, and is also in the same tuning, albeit at a lower octave. Yes, the cello through its bow technique has the ability to sustain long notes, and the banjo has virtually no sustain, yet somehow cello music can sound wonderful on the tenor banjo, almost lute-like in character. Of course, early tenor banjoists, under the influence of the mandolin, very often employed the tremolo technique to sustain a melodic line or single note, sometimes chords too. But tremolo is a "like it or loathe it" effect, and can be too much for some modern tastes. I therefore refuse to be dogmatic about it; if you like it, use it, if you don't, don't. It is not necessary for most classical music, but can occasionally be just what the moment demands. I personally use it very sparingly as an ornament, as you will hear on the sound files which accompany this edition.

[1] For an excellent and succinct overview, see https://www.banjohangout.org/article/7

The mandolin and mandola are the closest cousins of the tenor banjo, more so the latter with its CGDA tuning. They do however have four pairs of high-tension strings, and although there were attempts to emulate this on the mandolin-banjo, most players seemed to favor the adoption of single strings on the tenor banjo. The mandolin does, though, have a long and high-quality historical repertoire from the likes of Vivaldi, Mozart, Beethoven and others, and these works sit equally well on the tenor banjo, though the longer string length of the banjo might require some left-hand rethinking on occasion.

Of course, the mandolin/mandola was (mostly) played with a plectrum or pick, and therefore many early tenor banjoists migrated from a mandolin-family background. Mandolin quartets and quintets would perform recitals of the classical string quartet repertoire—a hugely ambitious undertaking—and I see no reason why the banjo family could not do likewise.

Early in the mandolin's history there is evidence that tremolo was used, but only occasionally. During the late Romantic period into the early 20th century, tremolo became an almost constant presence, as in the works of Ranieri and Calace. The choice of whether to emulate that fairly constant tremolo technique is yours alone.

After you have worked through this book, you might want to take on the extremely virtuoso music of Raffaele Calace, such as his "Ten Preludes for Mandolin" – music of the highest quality. If Bach is your thing, then his entire solo cello and violin music awaits. There is enough there to keep you occupied for the remainder of your life, no matter how long you live. But I hope that you will explore playing with other classical musicians, forging new pathways for the tenor banjo!

Composers and Sources

"Seven Pieces" by Robert Crome (c.1705 - c.1770) - The English cellist, Robert Crome, wrote one of the earliest cello methods in 1765, for the generation after the death in 1750 of J. S. Bach. This music is often described as "galant", very much simplified when compared to late Baroque music, yet tuneful and elegant. Interestingly, Crome recommends student cellists should add metal frets to the cello fingerboard, filing them flat when confidence in finger placement is achieved, leaving flush frets, which were often seen on 19th-century banjos.

"Nine Exercises" by Carlo Alfredo Piatti (1822 - 1901) - Although Piatti's cello method carries his name, most of the compositions are by other players, such as Romberg, Lee, Kummer, and Dotzauer, which could account for the popularity of this cello method. The pieces are relatively simple on the tenor banjo, but are tuneful and enjoyable to play.

"Three Minuets" by Giovanni Fouchetti (1757 - 1789) - from one of the earliest mandolin methods (Paris, 1771). The three minuets fit superbly well on the tenor banjo. Fouchetti wrote at a time when the *mandoline* (as it was called) could be played with a plectrum or with the fingers, and the number of strings could be four or six.

"De la Reine de Golconde" by Pietro Denis (1720 - 1790) - another excellent French mandolinist, Denis published two methods, one in 1768, the other in 1792. This theme with two variations is drawn from his first method.

"Two Pieces" by Niccolo Ceccherini (fl.1700) - composed for the four double-string baroque mandola in 1703. Ceccherini was a chamber musician at the court of the Grand Prince of Tuscany, Ferdinando de' Medici. This music will introduce you to the playing of two-part chords, which is a very useful technique to master. Take your time.

"Four Exercises" by Jean-Louis Duport (1749 1819) - These excellent studies come from Duport's "Essai sur le doigté du violoncelle et sur la conduite de l'archet" ("Essay on the fingering of the violoncello and on the conduct of the bow") of 1806, and they sound superbly well on the tenor banjo. You might want to experiment with different down and up strokes with the plectrum in the arpeggio studies.

"Two Pieces" by Fernando Sor (1778 - 1839) - Among his many accomplishments as operatic and symphonic composer, Fernando Sor also wrote many pieces for the guitar. These two studies are from his Opus 60 (Paris, 1837), and consist of only a single line. Try to hear the underlying chords, and double check those rhythms.

"Three Studies" by David Popper (1843 - 1913) - from his "Fünfzehn leichte melodisch-rhythmische Etüden", these are indeed "easy melodic-rhythmic studies". Although from a much later period (late 19th century) these studies will prepare you well for Bach's flute sonata (see below).

"Two Pieces" by Carl Fischer (1849 - 1923) - two interesting studies here. The first is concerned with position shifting on the inner two strings, while the second is concerned with phrasing a melody out of a continuous run of sixteenth notes, something which again will stand you in good stead when taking on Bach's flute music below.

"Study" by Raffaele Calace (1863 - 1934) - Arguably the greatest mandolin/mandola composer in history, and an absolute virtuoso performer, Calace also left an essential method for the mandolin (*Schule für Mandoline*, 1902) which I have called on for this study. Although not easy to play, this study is certainly a lot easier than his magnificent "10 Preludes" – so if you do find this piece easy, look for those preludes (I highly recommend the recording by Gertrud Troster). They will keep you occupied for a long time! As for this study, try to bring out the drama of each moment with varied dynamics, tone and tempi. Note that (typical for Romantic music on any string instrument) the high frets on all four strings are used, giving warmth and power to the soaring lines.

Solo Flute Sonata in Am by J. S. Bach (1685 - 1750) - We finish this book with music by J. S. Bach, starting with the superb sonata for solo flute, which fits perfectly on the tenor-banjo fretboard. The suite is unusual for Bach in that it lacks a prelude and gigue, and also because it is for solo flute. As the flute lacks the ability to play chords, the entire composition consists of a single line, yet chords and counterpoint are hinted at throughout. My preferred way of interpreting Bach's music is to imagine you are allowing the audience to eavesdrop on a conversation, and a very interesting one at that. Let the music breathe and carve out phrases, rather than playing first note to last without taking a breath

From the *5th Cello Suite* by J. S. Bach [in CGDG tuning] - These two pieces are very beautiful on cello, and no less so on tenor banjo. The Allemande is a German dance of slow to medium pace. The slow Sarabande is deceptively simple. Aim for beautiful tone and phrasing. Note the tuning: the first string is tuned down from A to G. This is the tuning Bach used on the cello. By the way, when we mention cello in connection with Bach's cello suites, there is growing evidence that the cello he had in mind – the *violoncello da spalla* (shoulder cello) – was an overgrown viola, which was held under the chin, very different indeed from the standard cello. This lowered tuning allows interesting chord formations.

How to Use This Book

No matter what your level, start at the beginning. For some, that will be their actual technical level. For more advanced players, use the first pieces to develop tone and phrasing. Most students are hindered by playing music that is too difficult for them, but playing easier pieces well, musically, is better than always attempting music beyond your technical level.

Classical music needs to be shaped by the performer for it to sound at its best. Try experimenting with breathing spaces, carve out short phrases, imagine that while playing you are talking to someone through the music. When talking, you quite naturally emphasise some words, take breaths, raise and lower your voice, etc; music performance is no different. It is not simply a case of playing the right notes in the right order in the right time, and then moving on to the next piece.

These studies have been chosen to develop your musicianship, not just technique.

Download and listen to the free sound files – see the title page of the book for details – and notice, for example, where I place accents or let the music breathe. Interpretation is a fluid thing, and on another day I might offer a quite different interpretation.

Notation

It is much better to read standard notation than TAB. However, as a teacher with 30 years' experience, I am well aware that some very intelligent people just cannot compute standard notation, no matter how much time they put in or how hard they try. I do not want to exclude these people from making beautiful music. Even if you can read standard notation, it is sometimes helpful to glance at the TAB to see where on the fretboard I play the notes, which - for musical reasons - might not be the obvious place.

I typeset the scores with *MuseScore 3*, and one peculiarity it has in the TAB part is depicting a half note (minim) with two short lines through the stem. (See TAB for measure 4 of the first piece as an example.) Some editors use such a device to indicate tremolo, which is not the case in this book. Tremolo is something you can add at your own discretion; it is not indicated in the score.

I also encourage you to work out your own left-hand fingering, and to this end I have not included any guides. Try to find the smoothest way to connect notes, and over time you will develop a good sense of the most efficient and most musical fingering. I am asking a lot of you here, but with patience and commitment you can eventually learn to trust yourself, and that is a big part of becoming a mature musician.

Strings and Things

For classical playing, I very much prefer flat-wound strings, such as Thomastik-Infeld 1244.

Plectrums or picks: I have tried many kinds over the years, but keep coming back to Gibson EH (extra heavy). They are cheap and easily available, and I recommend a tin containing fifty of them.

The banjo I used for the recording is a Deering Sierra 19-fret tenor – highly recommended. But there is no specific instrument called a “classical tenor banjo”, and any tenor will do. For my Bach recording (*Bach’s Cello Suites I-III Arranged for Tenor Banjo*, Mel Bay 30430M) I used three very different instruments: Deering Eagle II Tenor, Gold Tone Cello Banjo CEB-4, and a gut-strung gourd tenor banza by Jason Smith of jaybirdbanjo.

The recording was made with a Rode NT-4 stereo mic into a Fostex FR2LE recorder.

Tuition

If you would like lessons in playing classical tenor banjo, I teach via *Zoom* from my studio in Edinburgh. See https://robmackillop.net for details.

Rob MacKillop
South Queensferry,
Edinburgh, 2021

Minuet in Am

Arranged by
Rob MacKillop

1

Compleat Tutor for the Violoncello 1765, p. 17

R. Crome

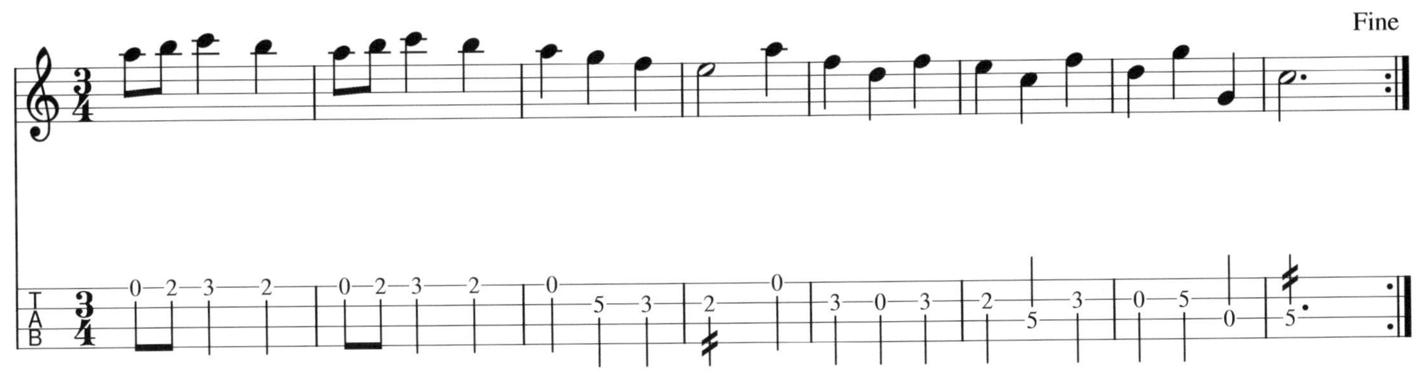

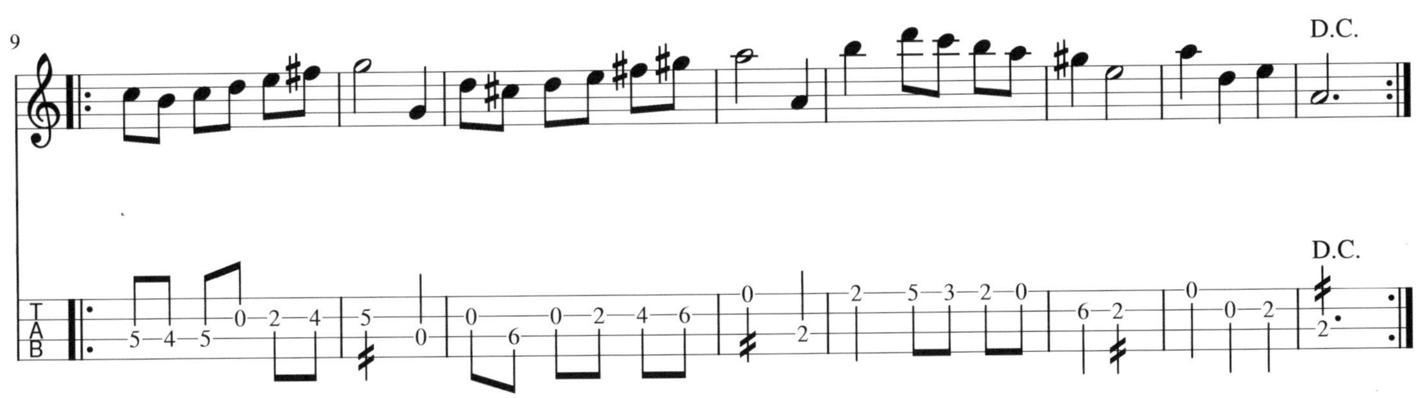

Jigg in Am

Arranged by
Rob MacKillop

Compleat Tutor for the Violoncello 1765, p. 17

R. Crome

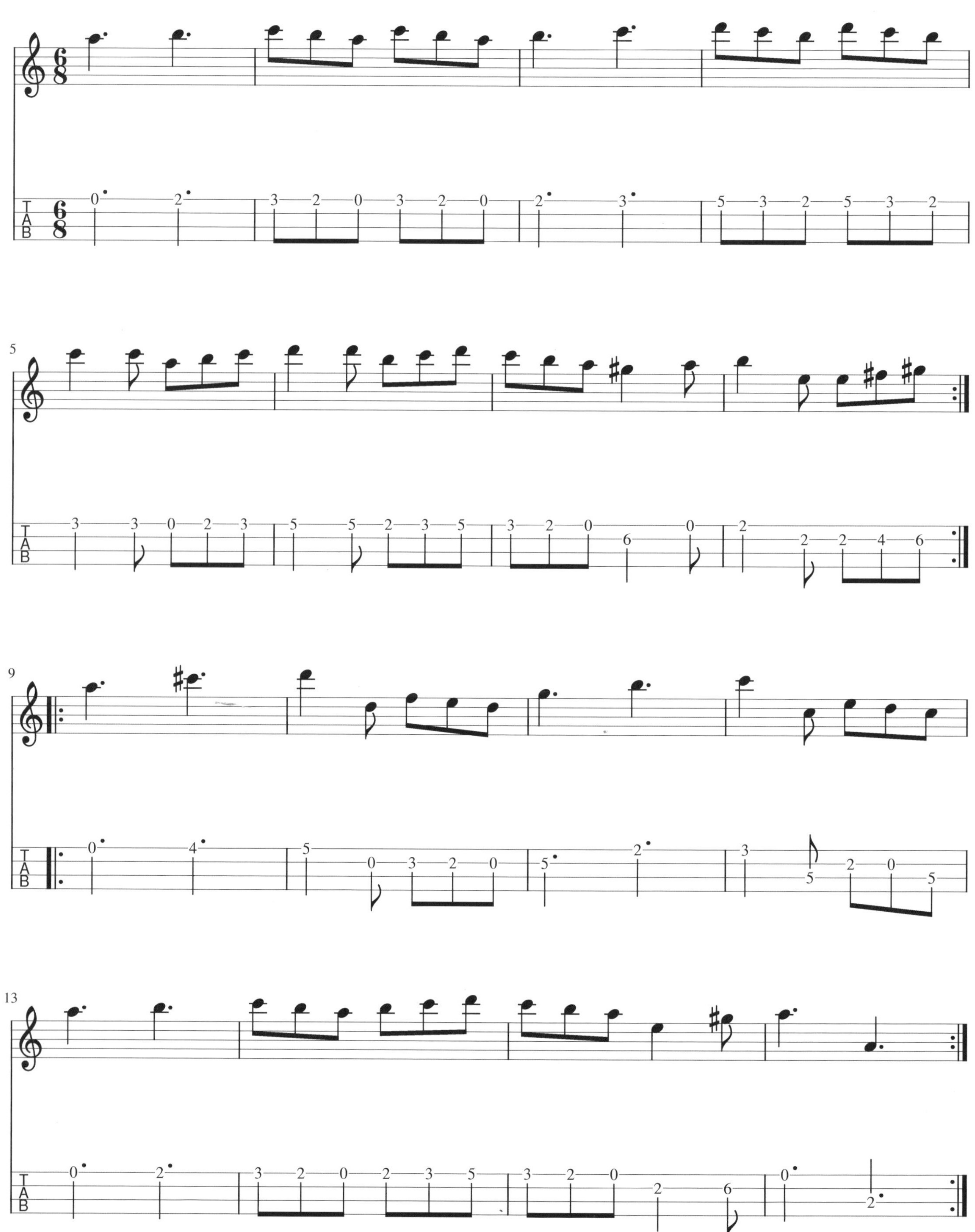

Minuet in C

Arranged by
Rob MacKillop

Compleat Tutor for the Violoncello 1765, p. 15

R. Crome

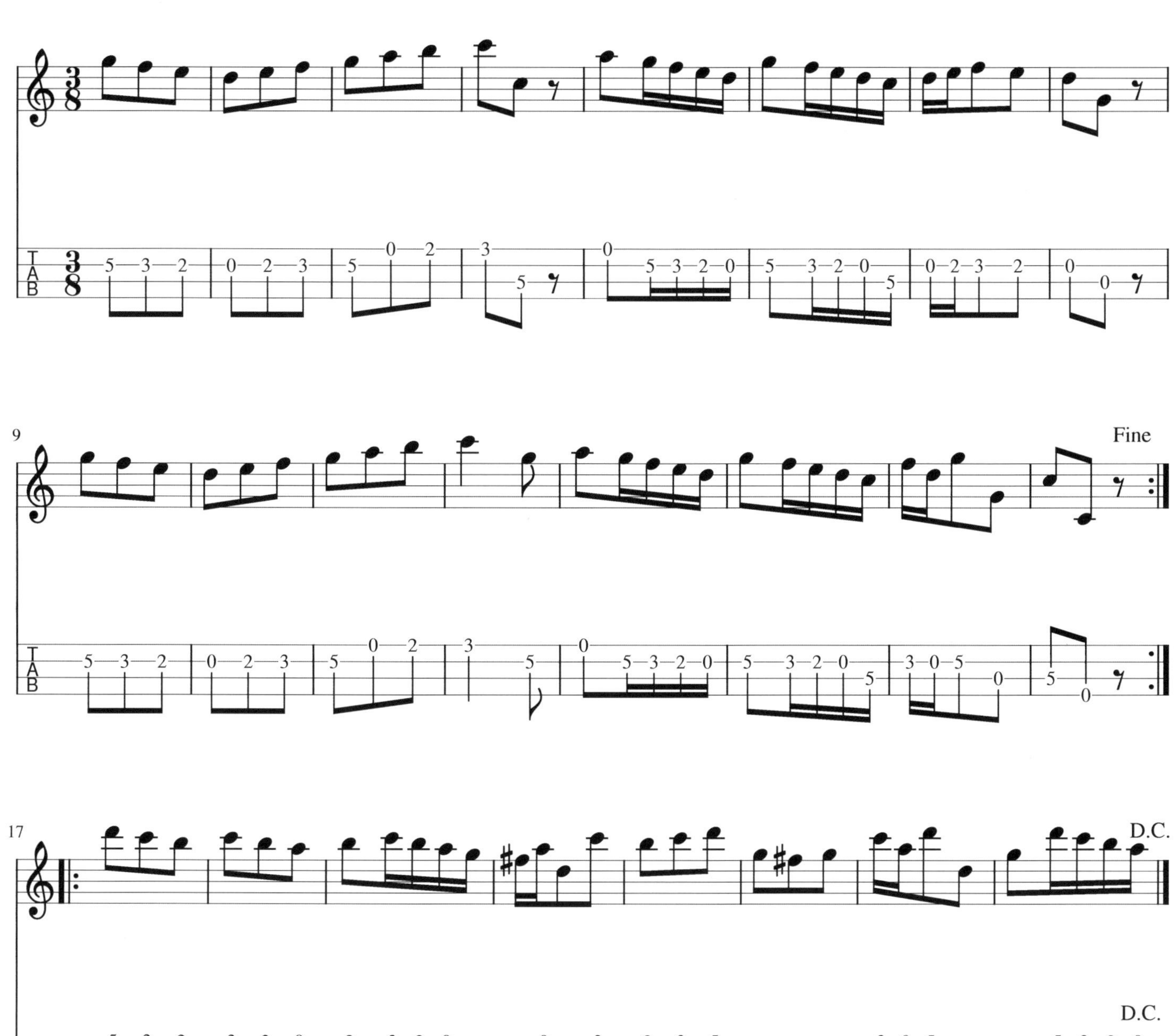

Minuet in F Major

Arranged by
Rob MacKillop

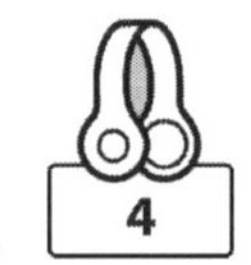

Compleat Tutor for the Violoncello 1765, p. 19

R. Crome

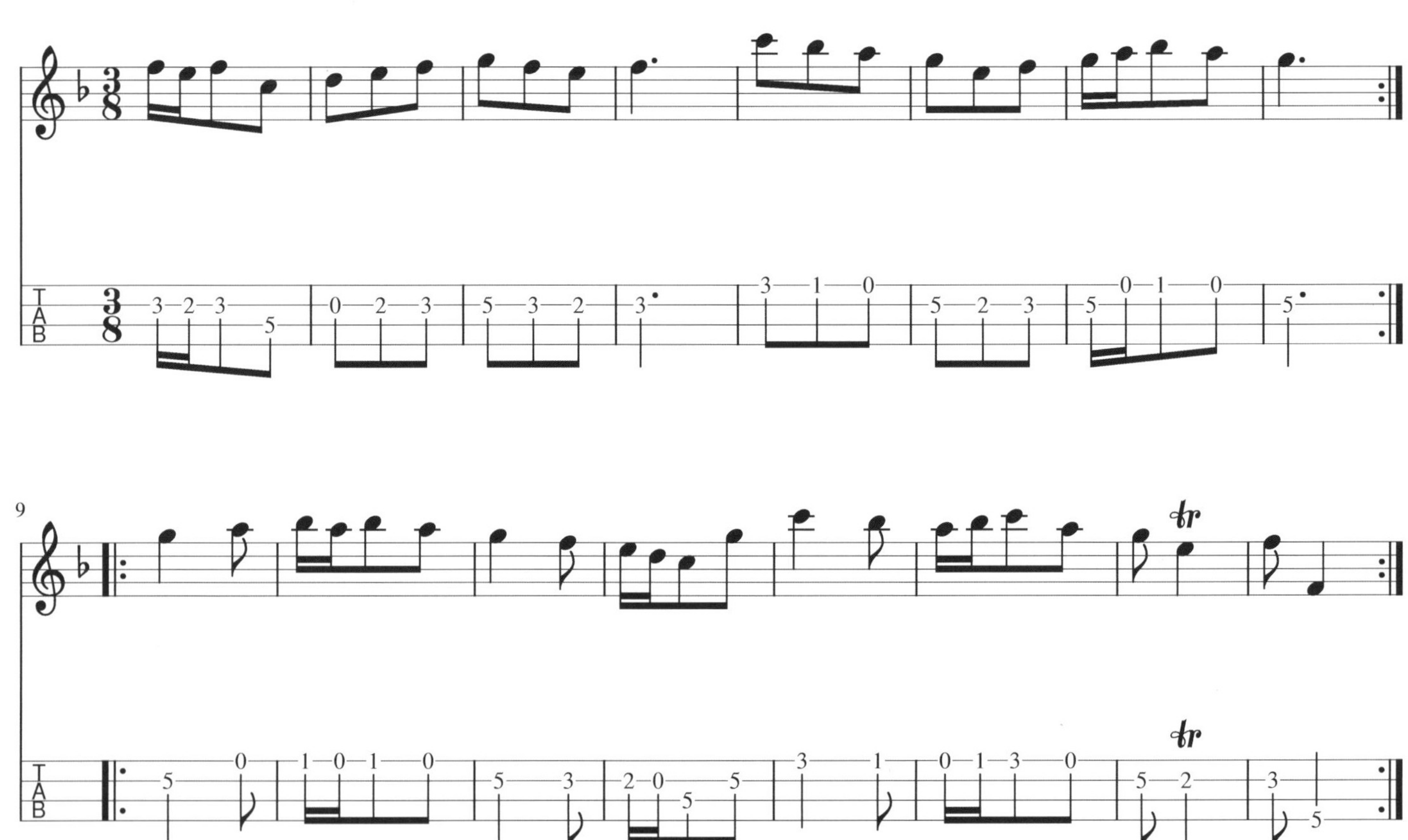

Jigg in G Major

Arranged by
Rob MacKillop

5

Compleat Tutor for the Violoncello 1765, p. 19

R. Crome

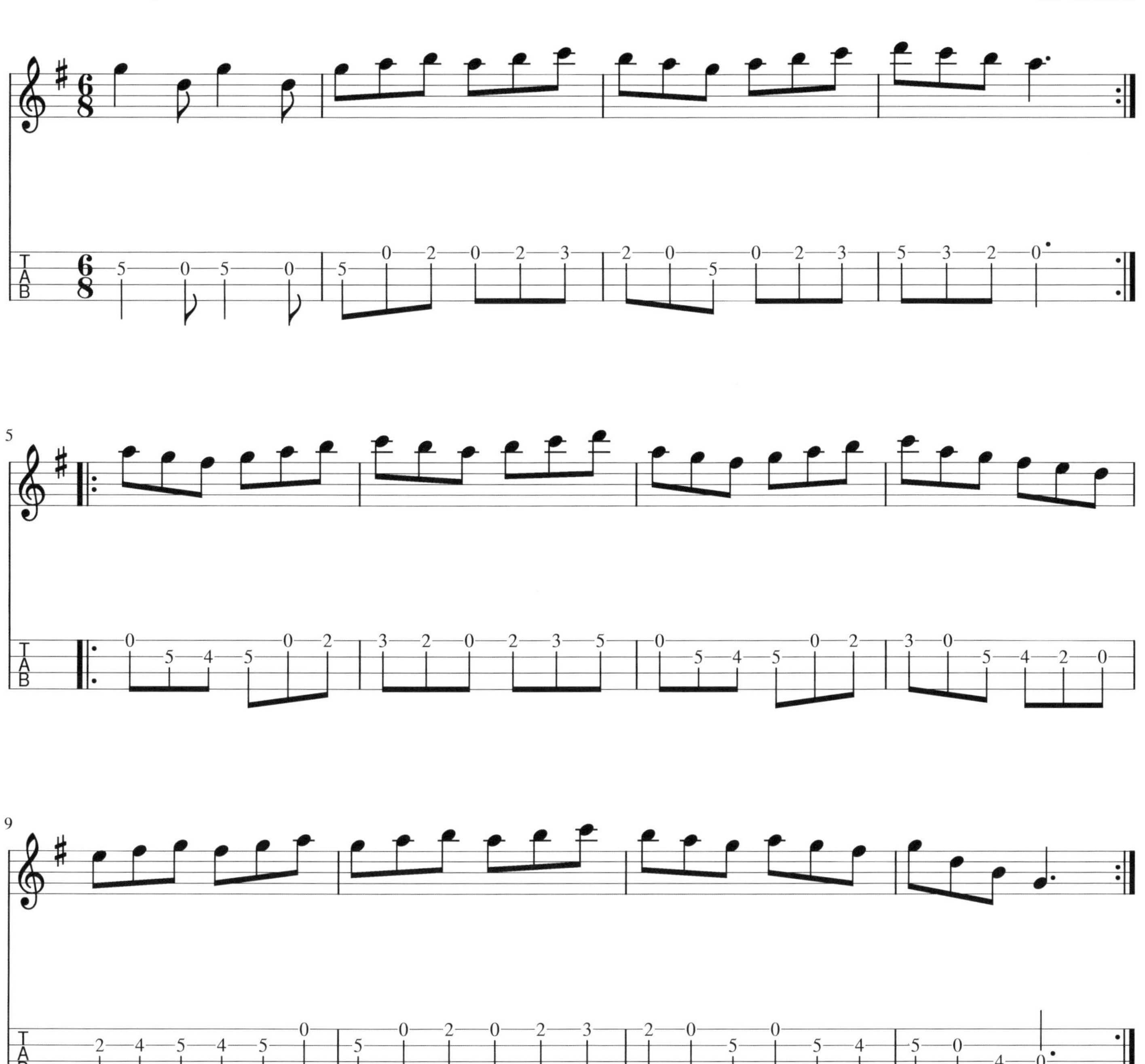

Gavot in C Major

Arranged by
Rob MacKillop

Compleat Tutor for the Violoncello 1765, p. 19

R. Crome

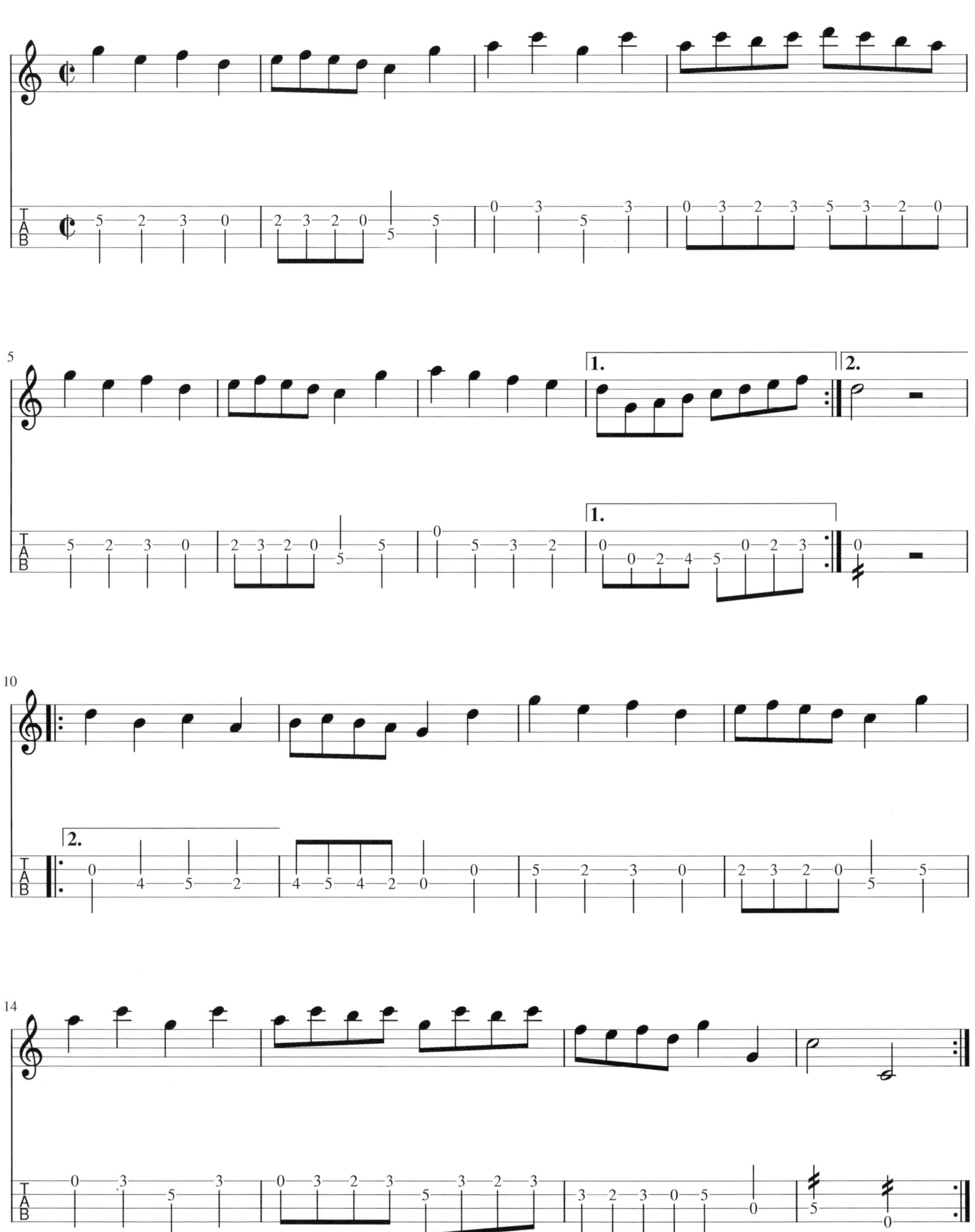

Minuet in A Major

Arranged by
Rob MacKillop

7

Compleat Tutor for the Violoncello 1765, p. 19

R. Crome

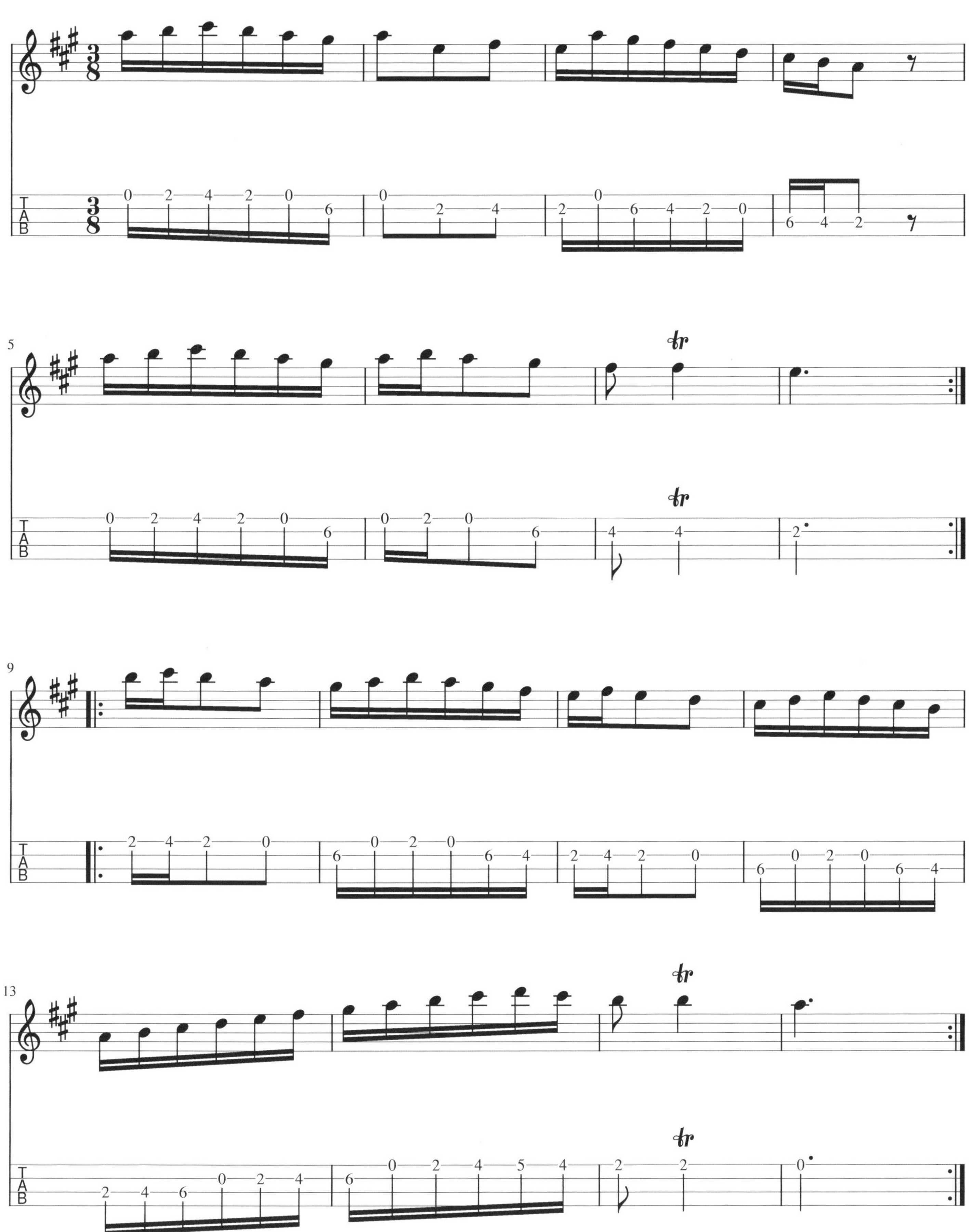

Exercise 1

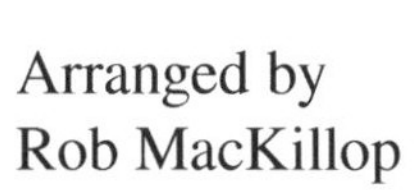

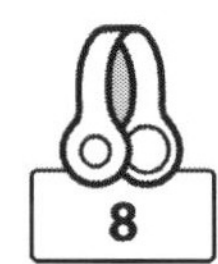

Methode de Violoncelle
by A. Piatti, 1882

Romberg

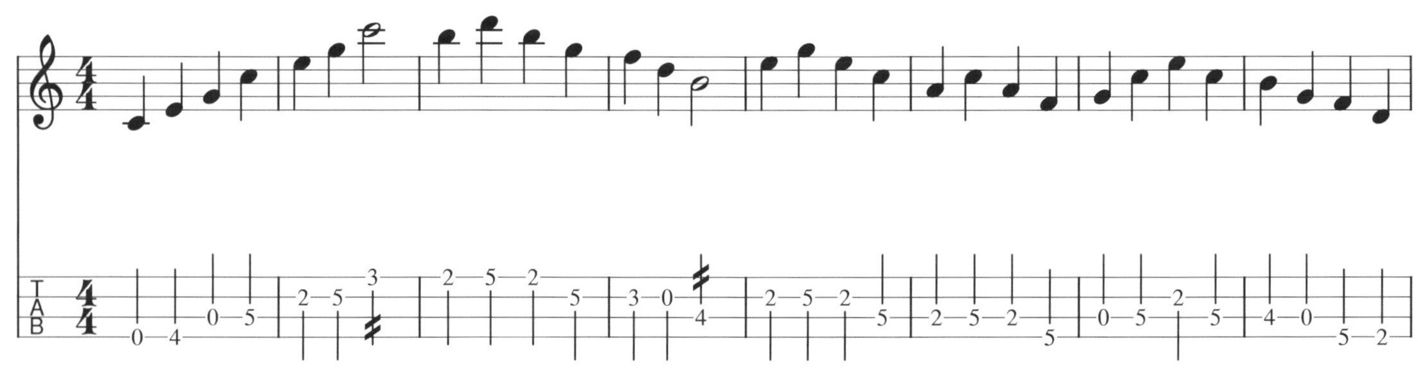

9

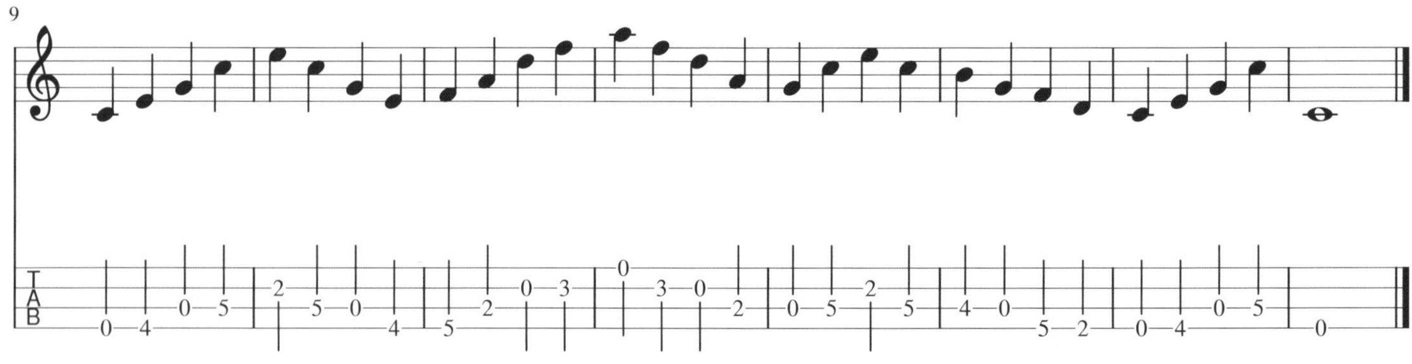

Exercise 2

Arranged by
Rob MacKillop

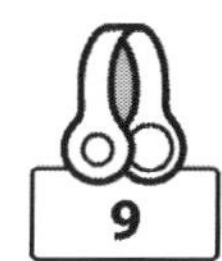

Methode de Violoncelle
by A. Piatti, 1882

Romberg

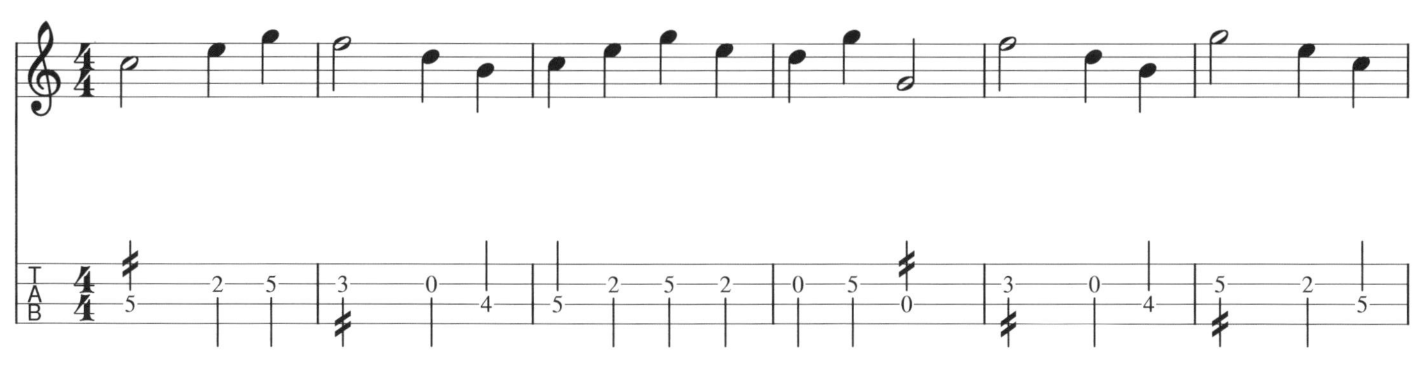

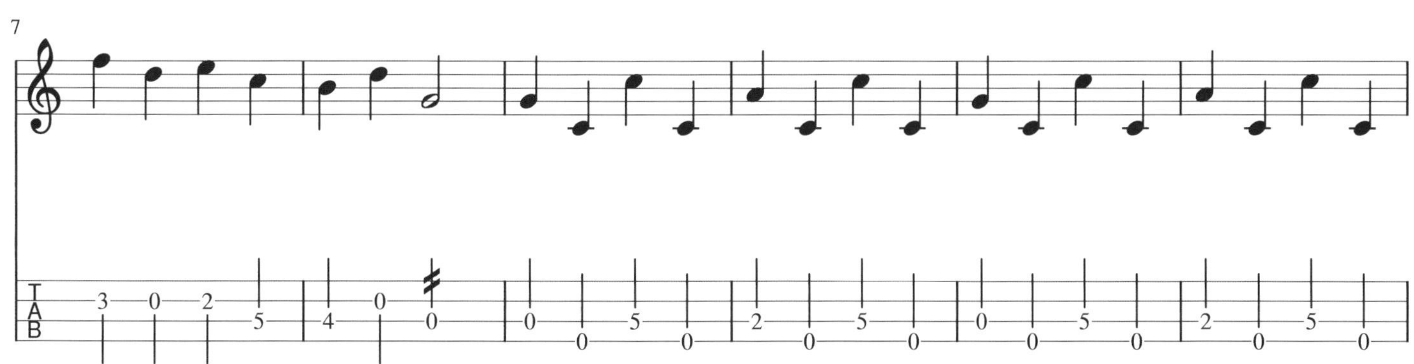

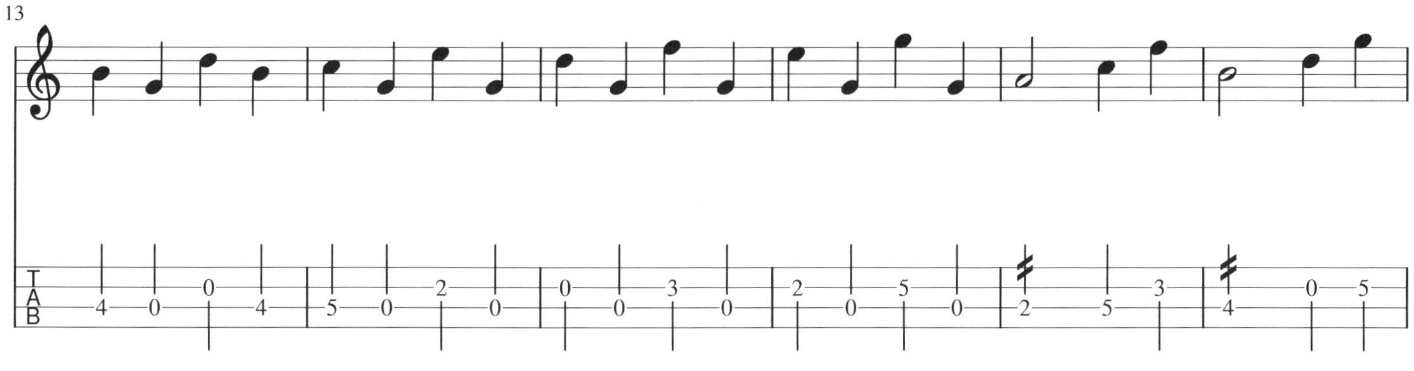

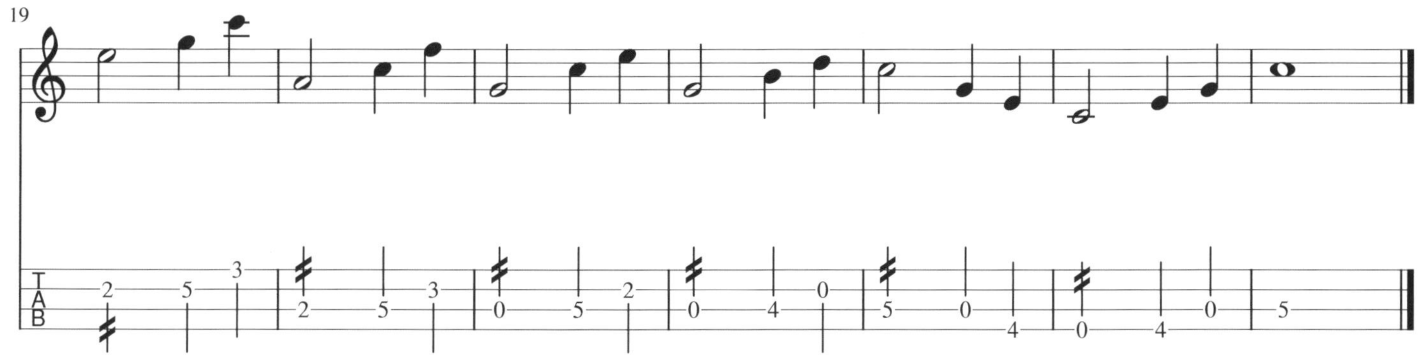

Exercise 3

Arranged by Rob MacKillop

10

Methode de Violoncelle
by A. Piatti, 1882

Lee

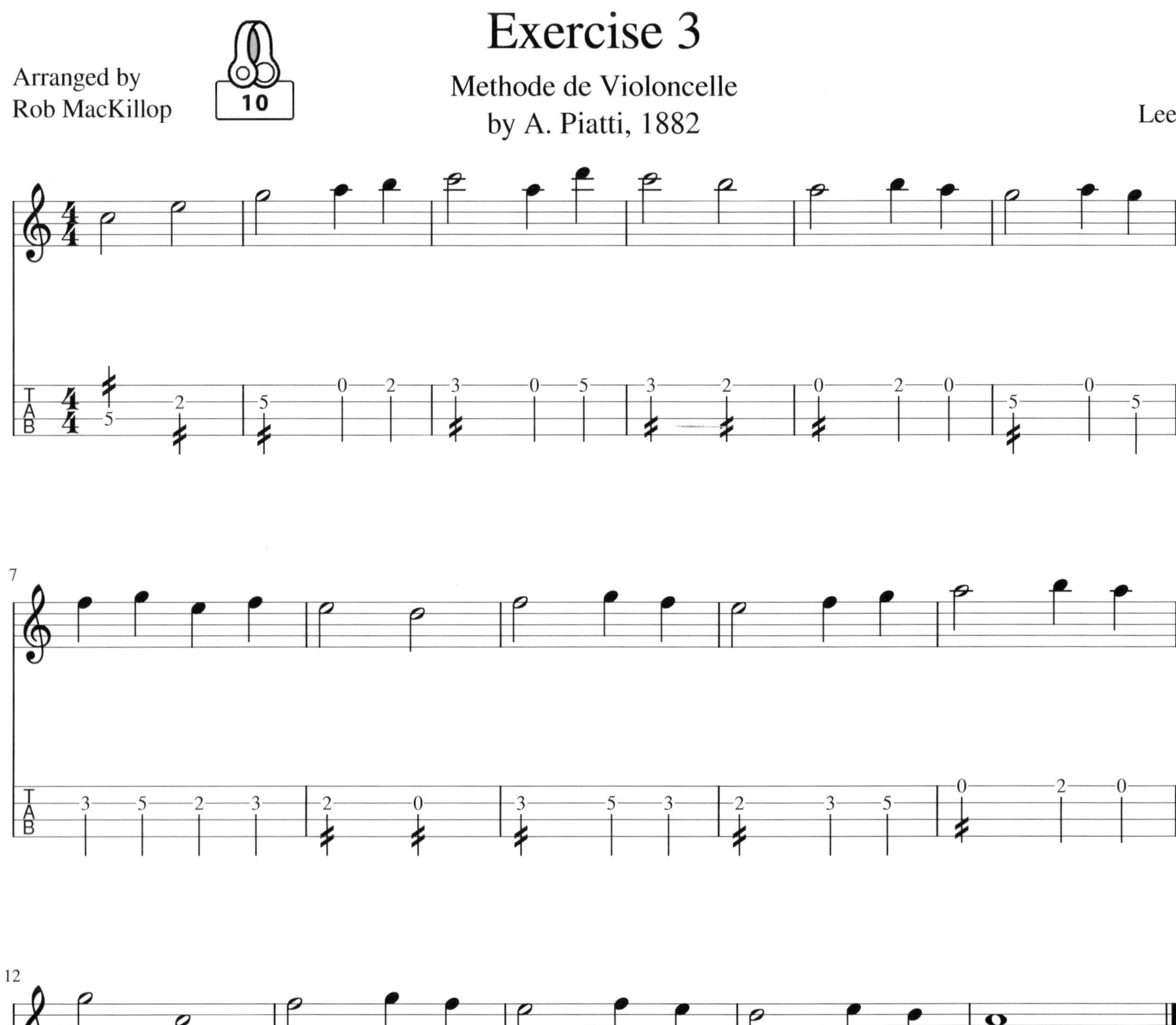

Exercise 5

Methode de Violoncelle
by A. Piatti, 1882

Arranged by
Rob MacKillop

Lee

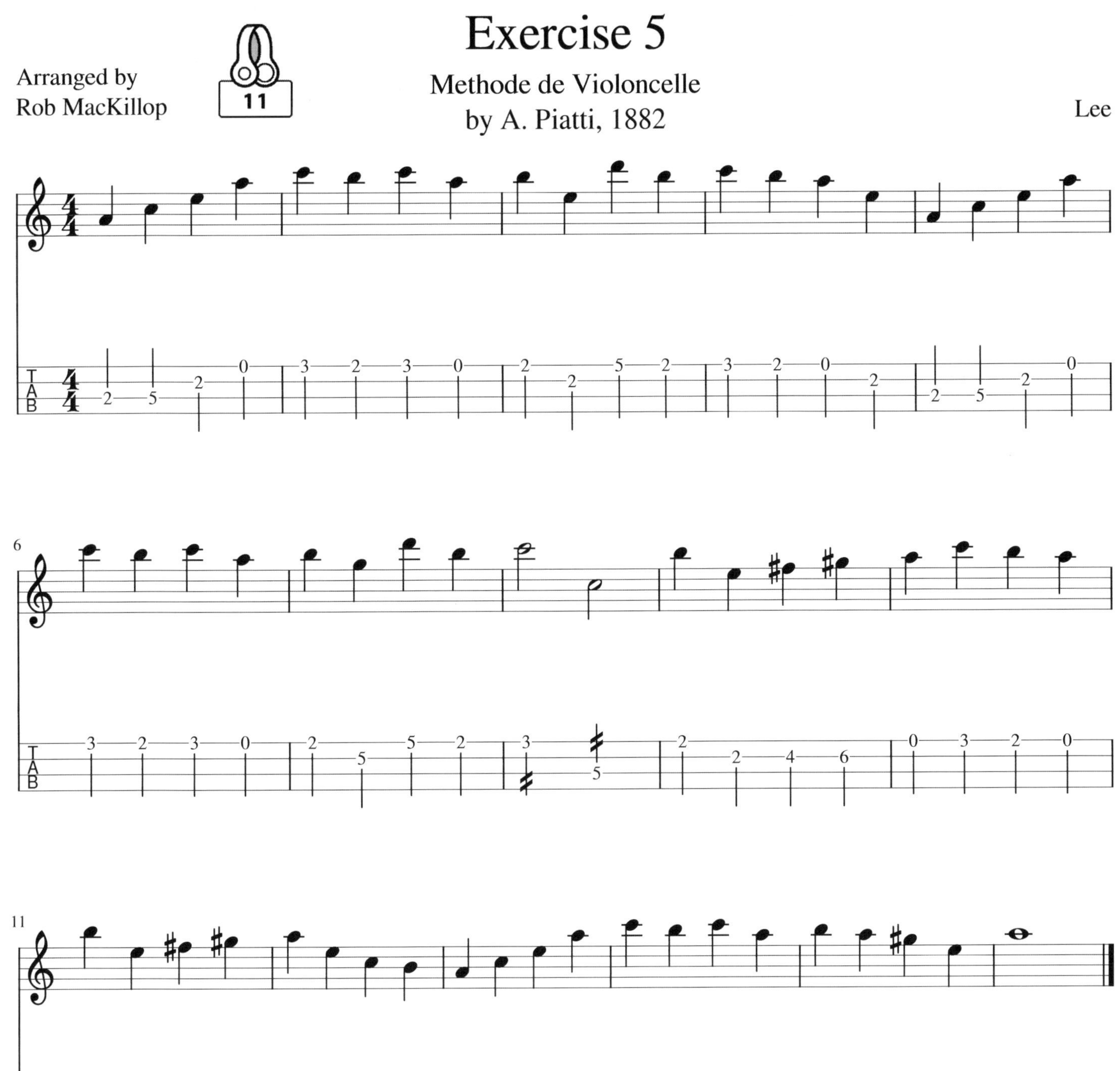

Exercise 7

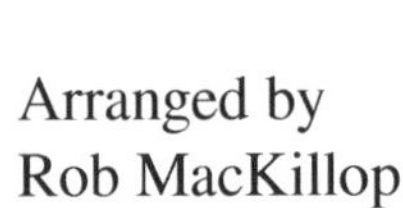

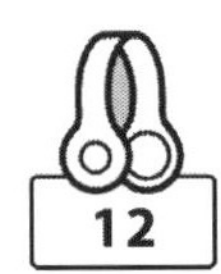

Methode de Violoncelle
by A. Piatti, 1882

Tabb

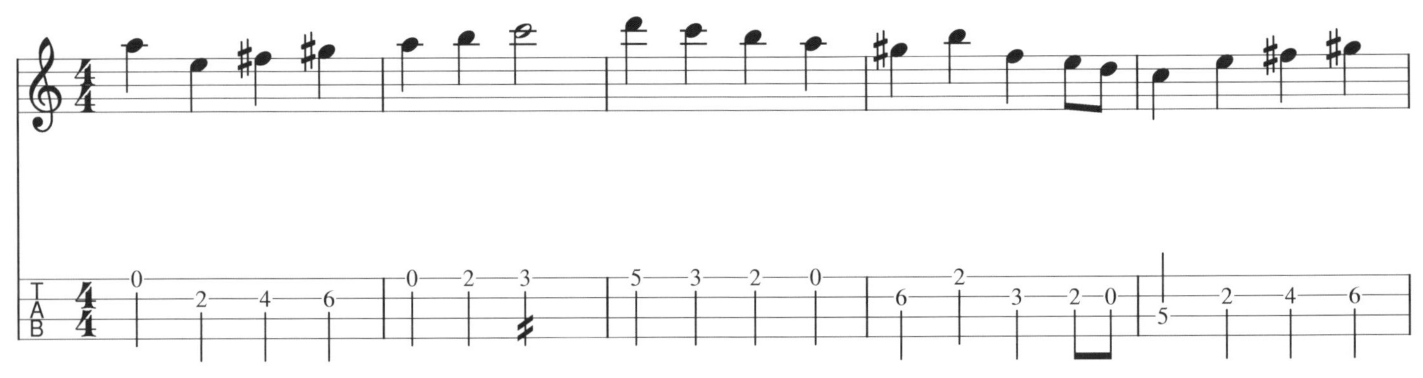

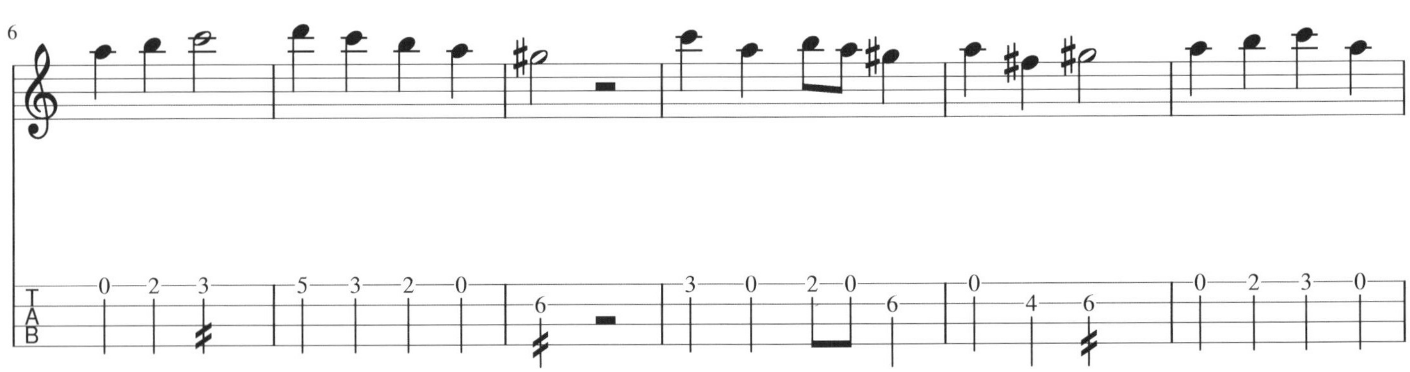

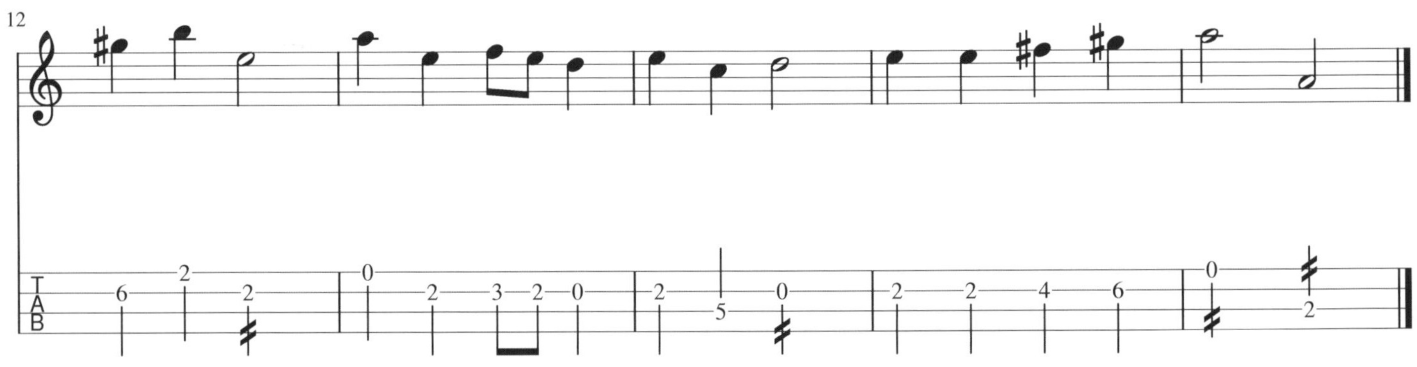

Exercise 14

Arranged by
Rob MacKillop

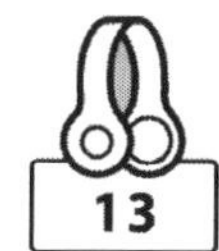

Methode de Violoncelle
by A. Piatti, 1882

Kummer

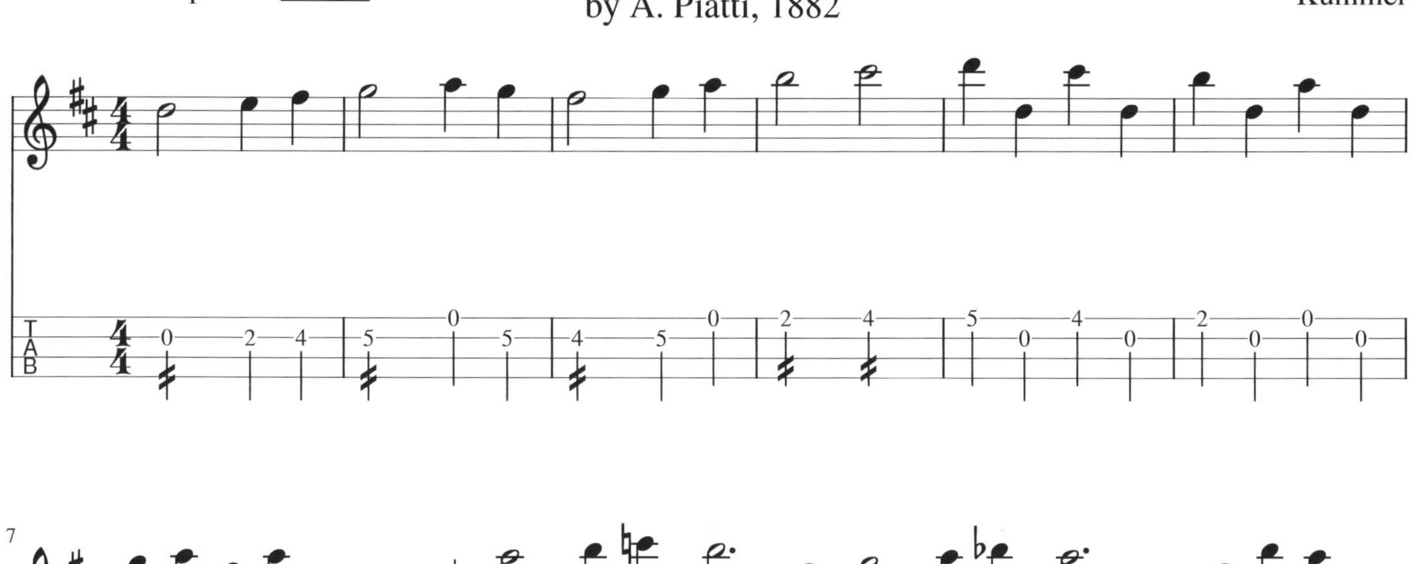

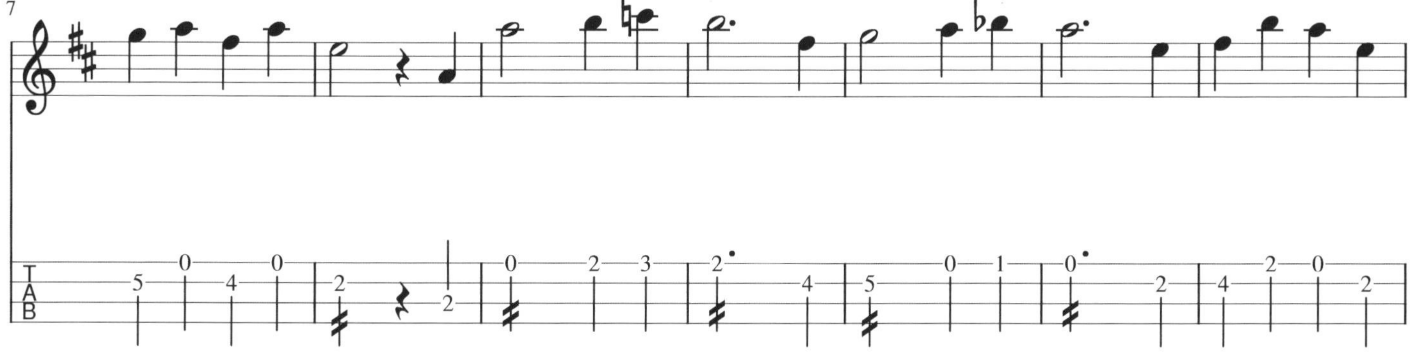

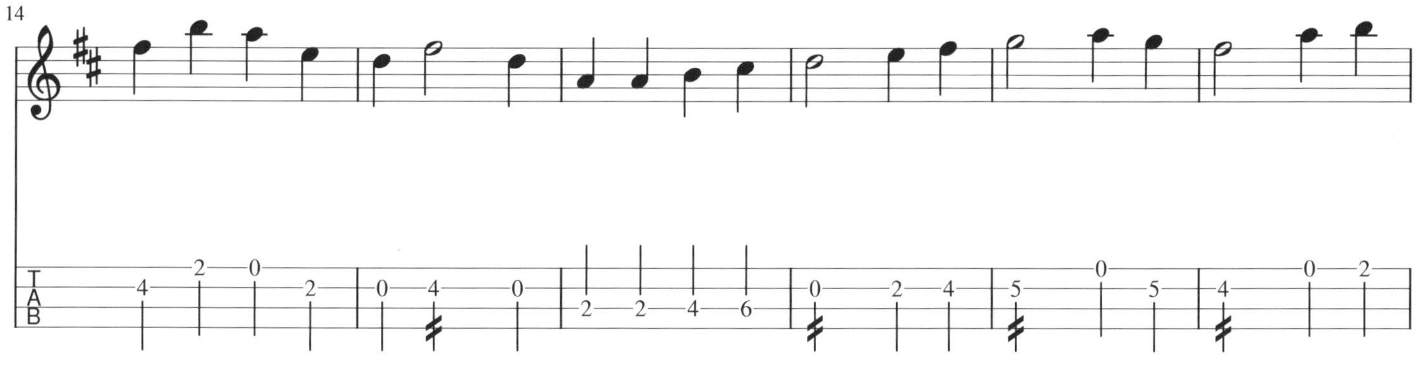

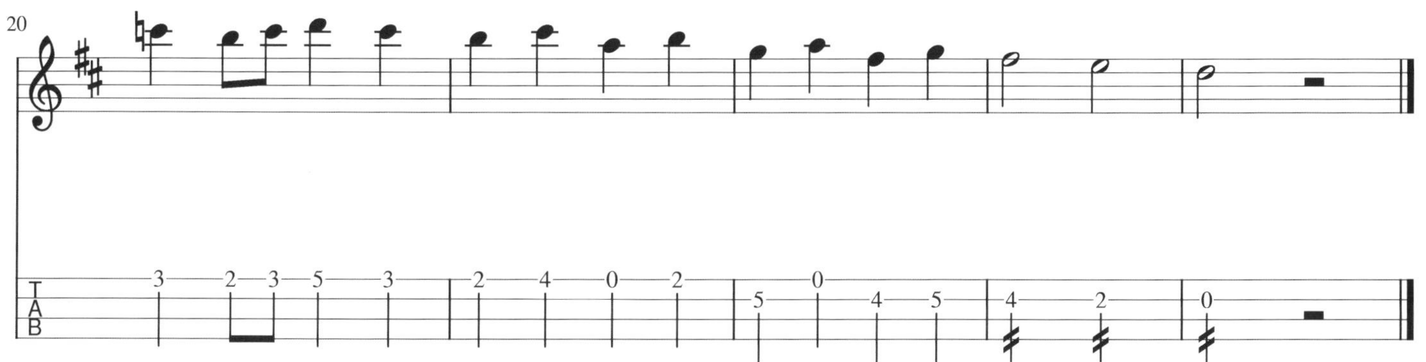

Arranged by
Rob MacKillop

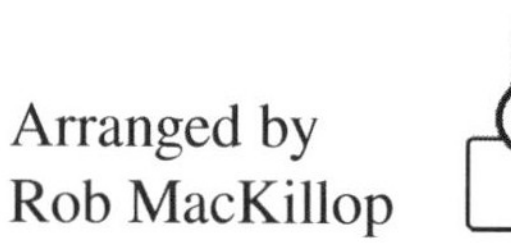

Exercise 17

Methode de Violoncelle
by A. Piatti, 1882

Dotzauer

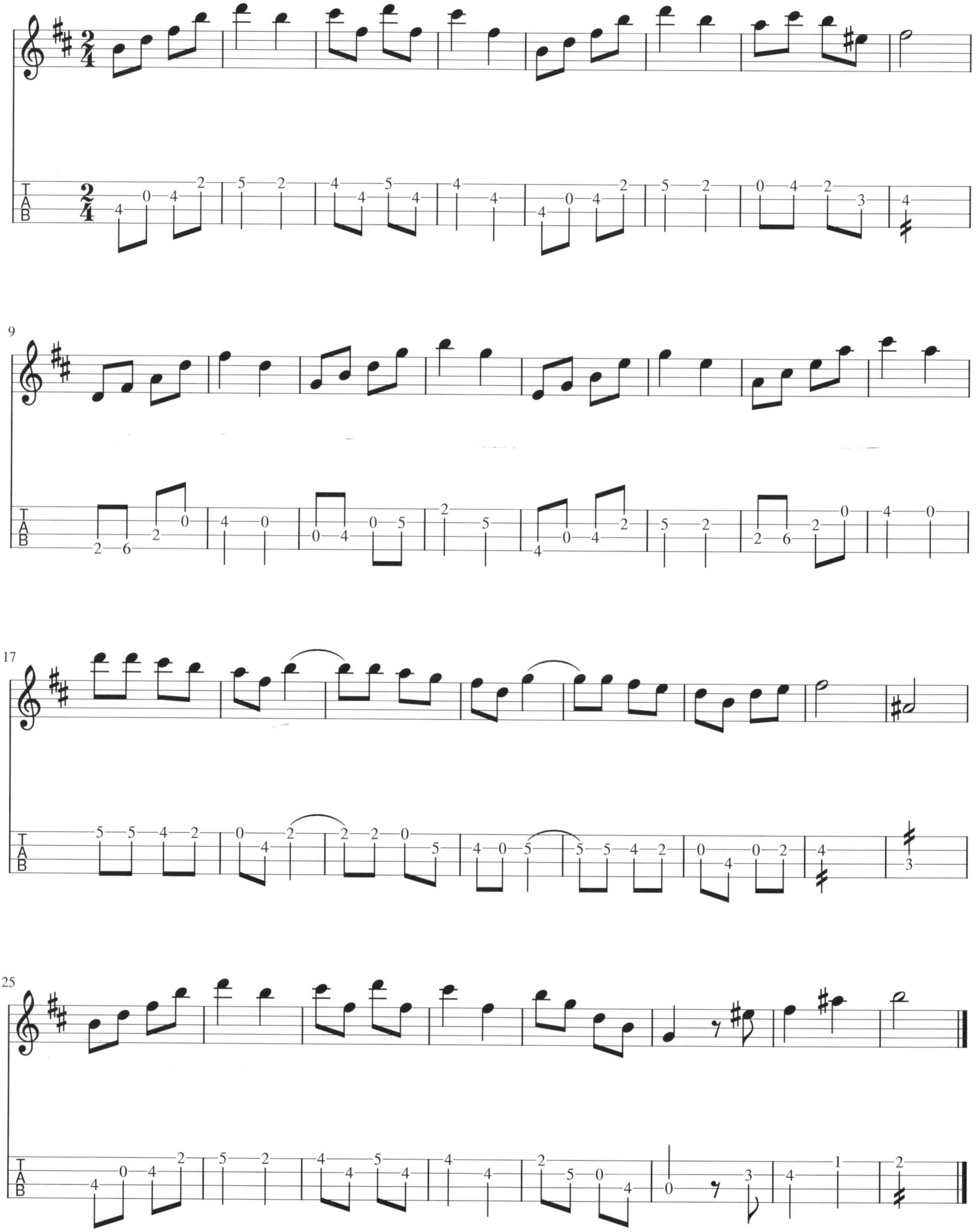

Exercise 23

Methode de Violoncelle
by A. Piatti, 1882

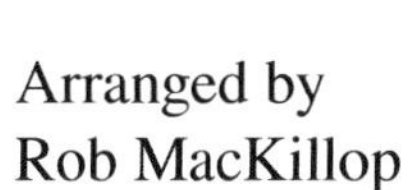

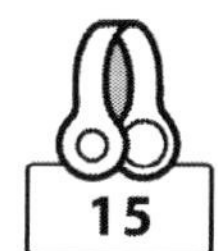

Kummer

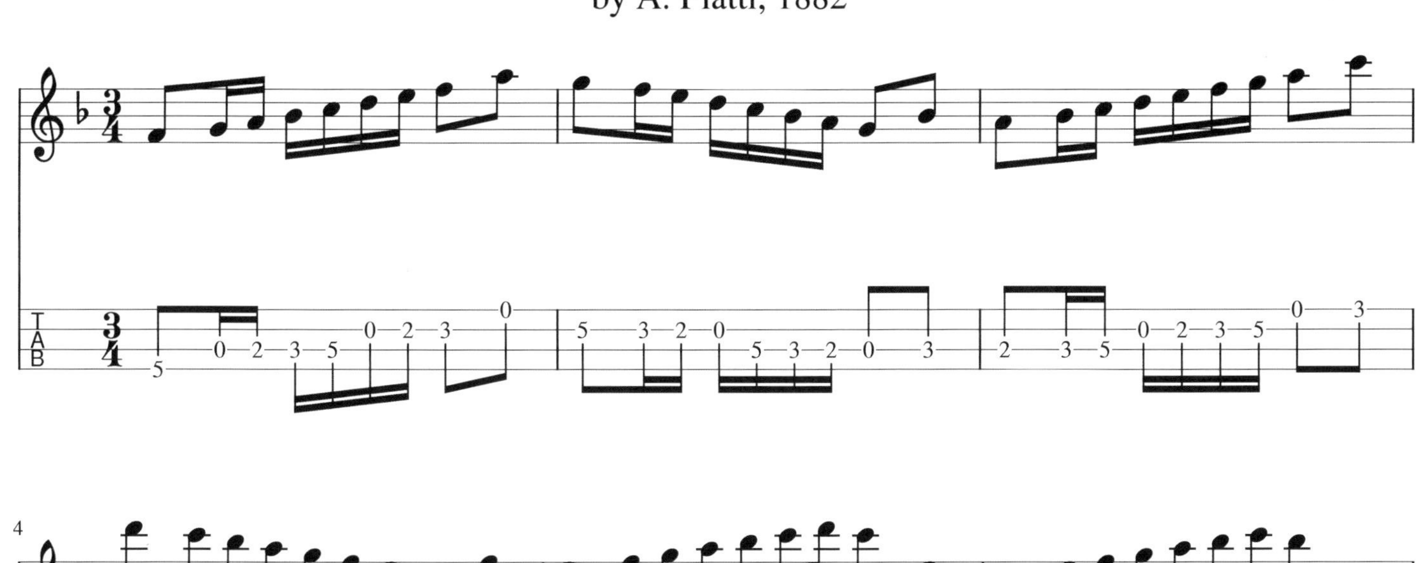

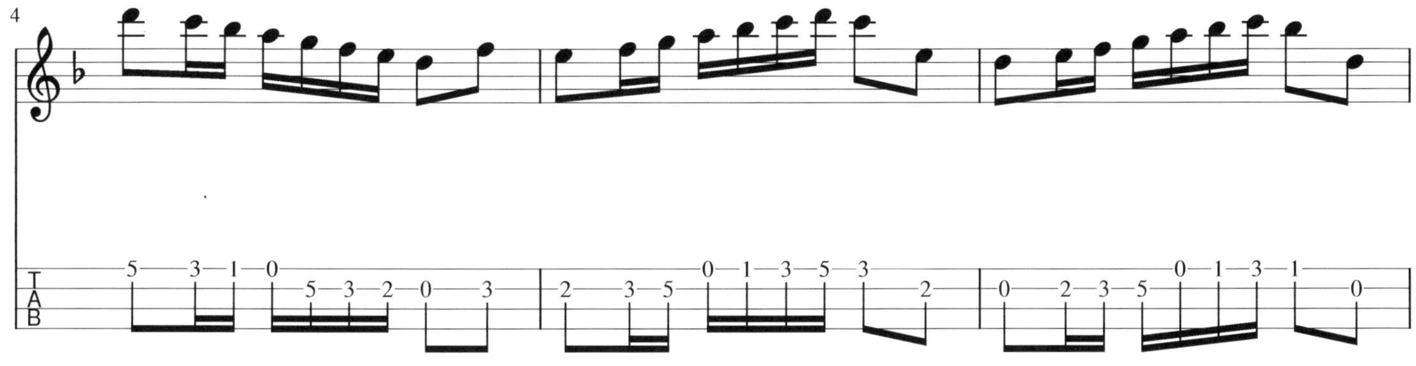

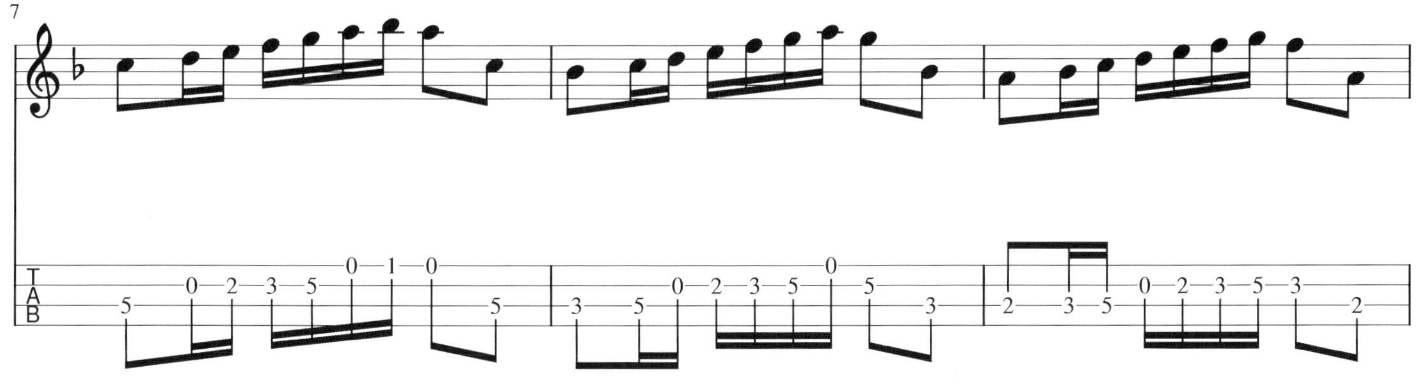

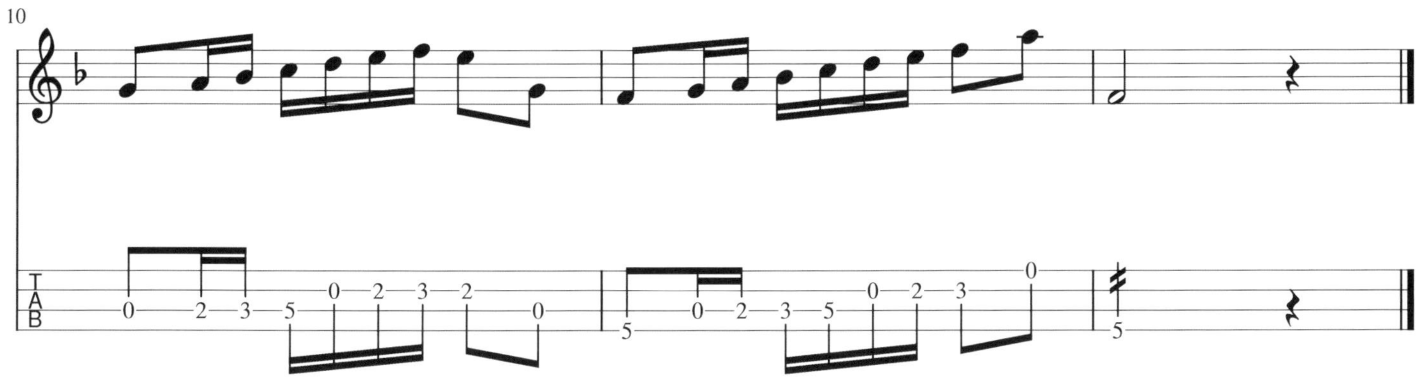

Exercise 29

Arranged by
Rob MacKillop

Methode de Violoncelle
by A. Piatti, 1882

Romberg

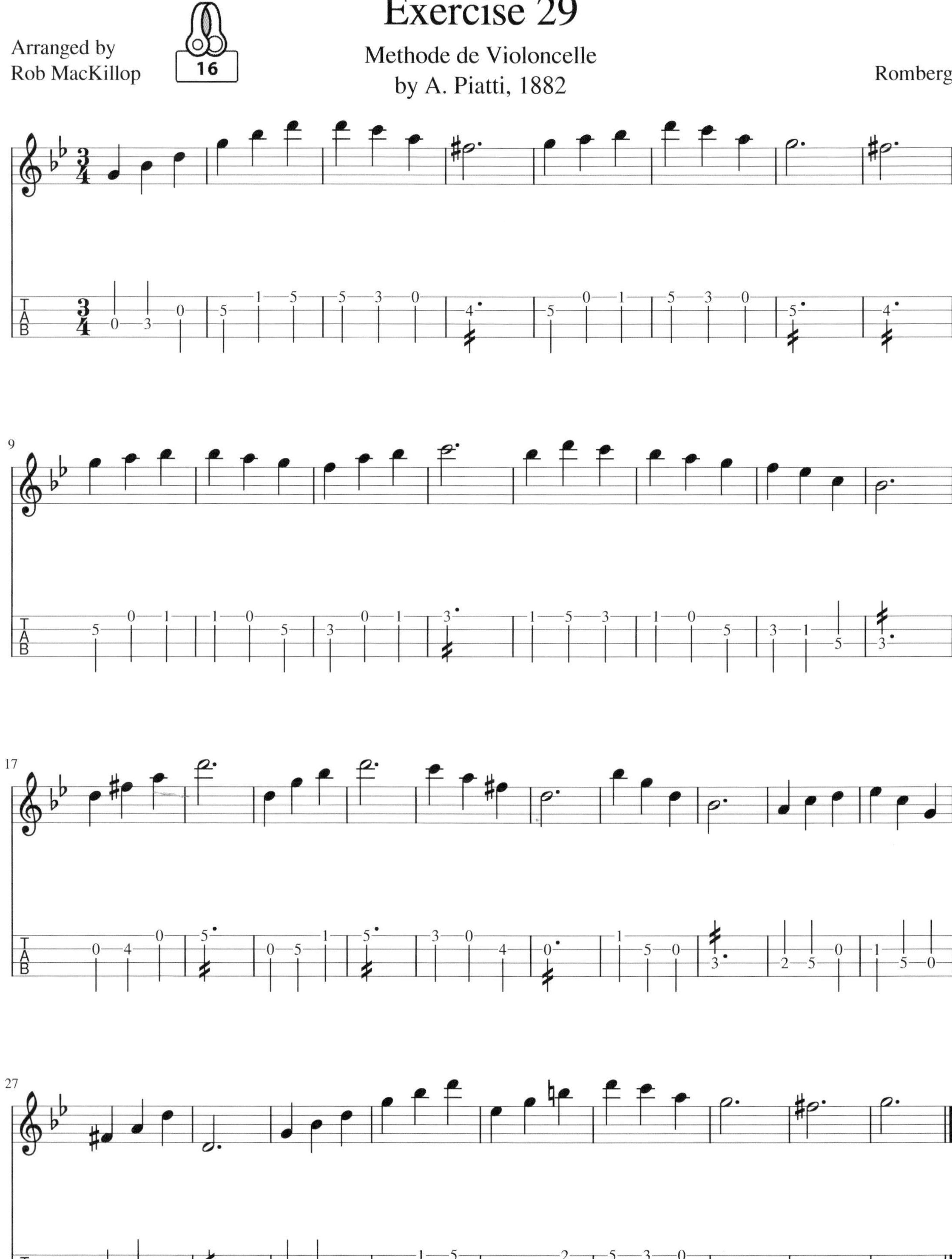

Minuetto (1)

Methode c.1771

Arranged by
Rob MacKillop

17

Giovanni Fouchetti
(1757 - 1789)

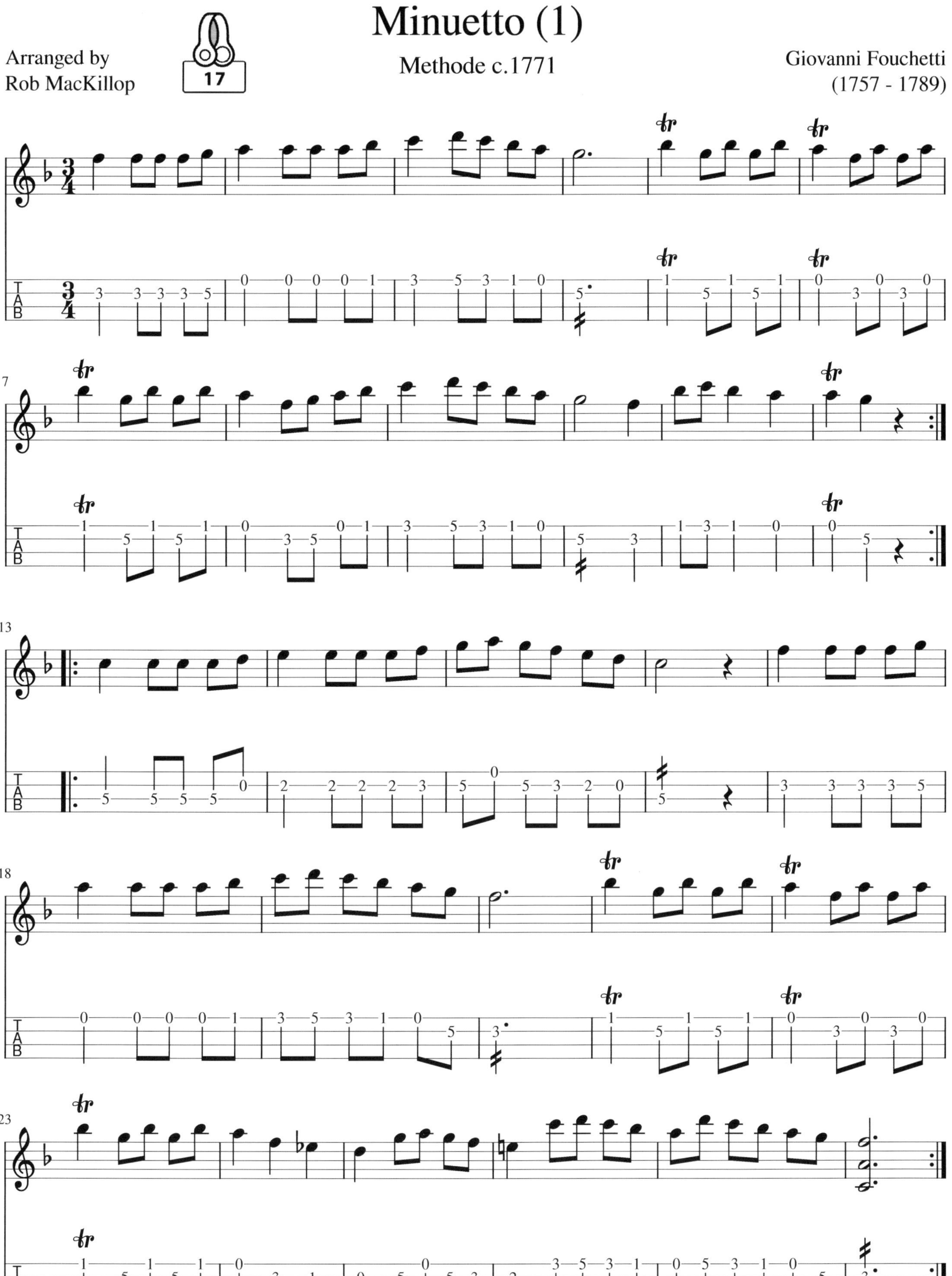

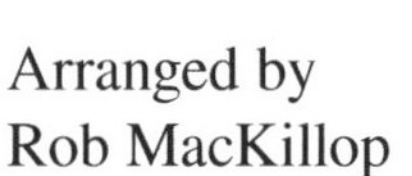

Minuetto (2)

Methode c.1771

Giovanni Fouchetti
(1757 - 1789)

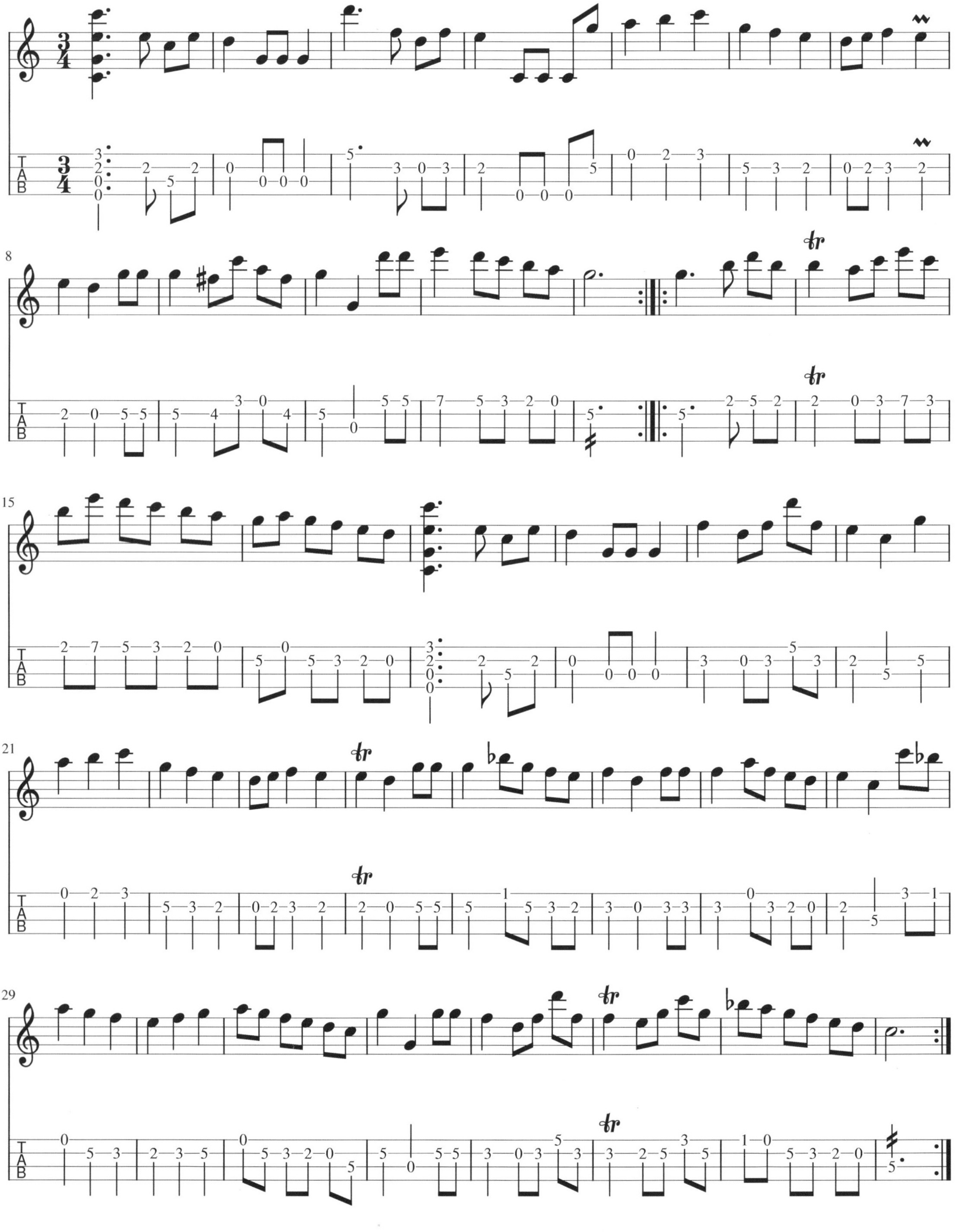

Minuetto (3)

Methode 1771

Arranged by
Rob MacKillop

19

Giovanni Fouchetti
(1757 - 1789)

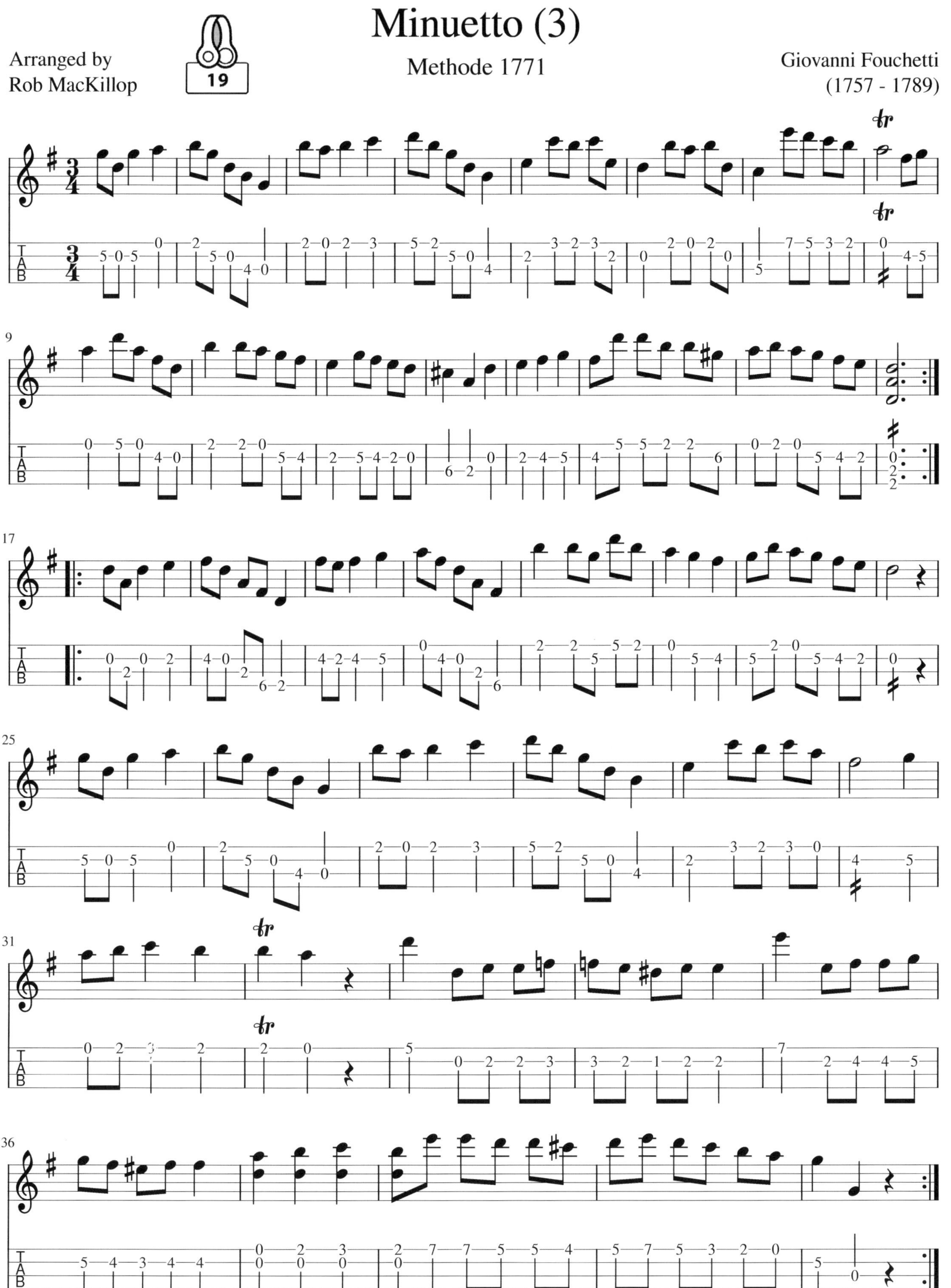

De la Reine de Golconde

Arranged by
Rob MacKillop

20

Methode Part II, p. 24

P. Denis

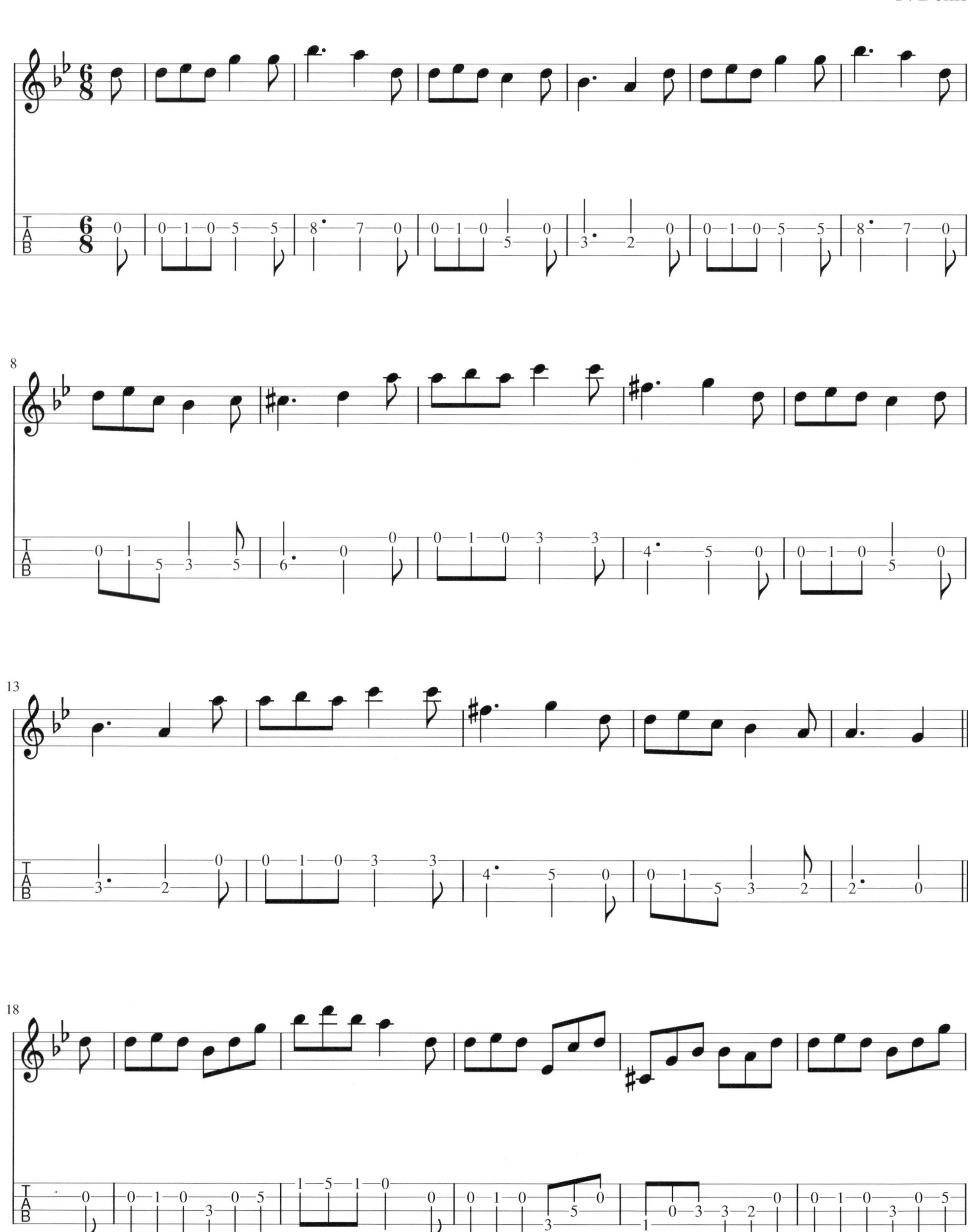

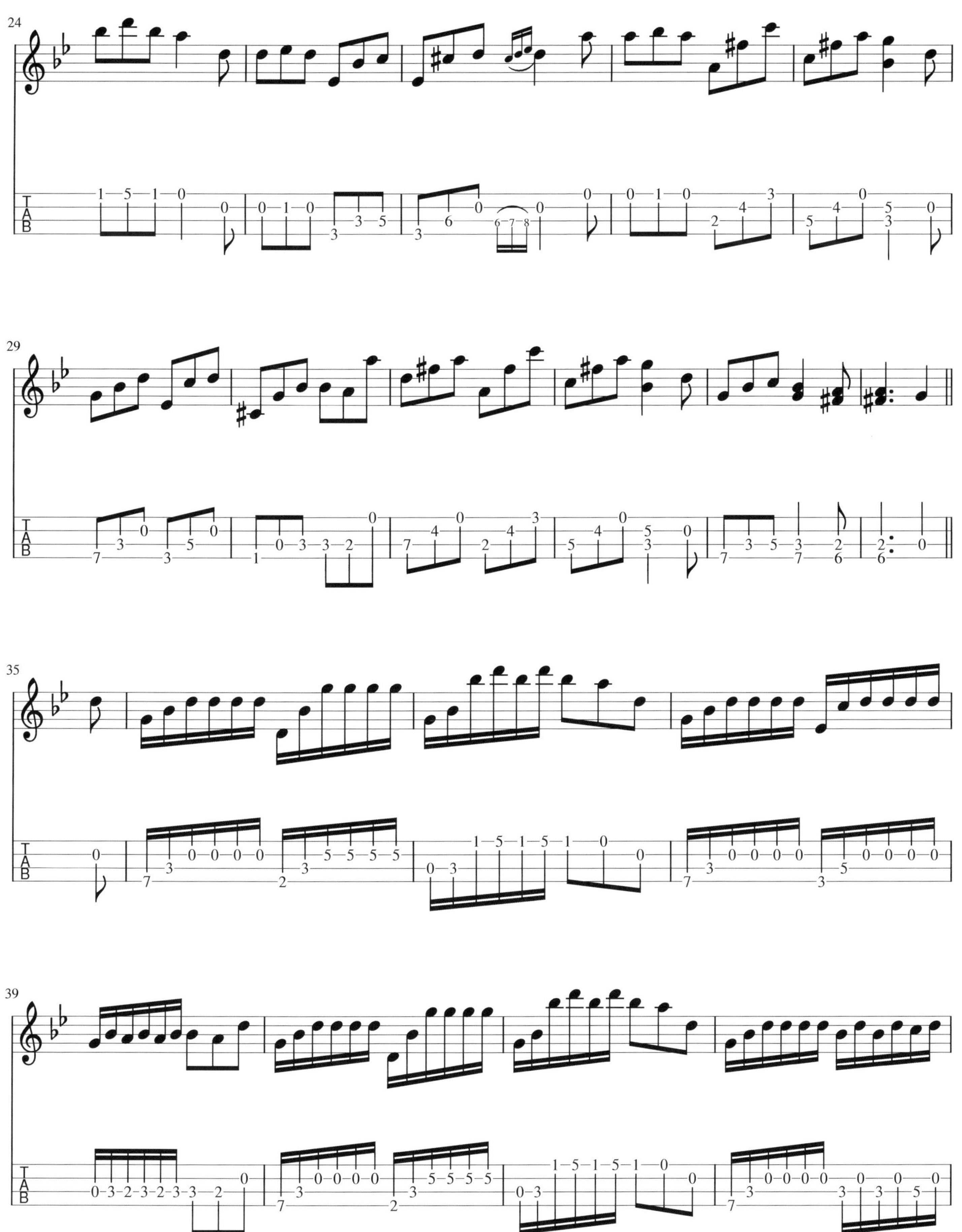

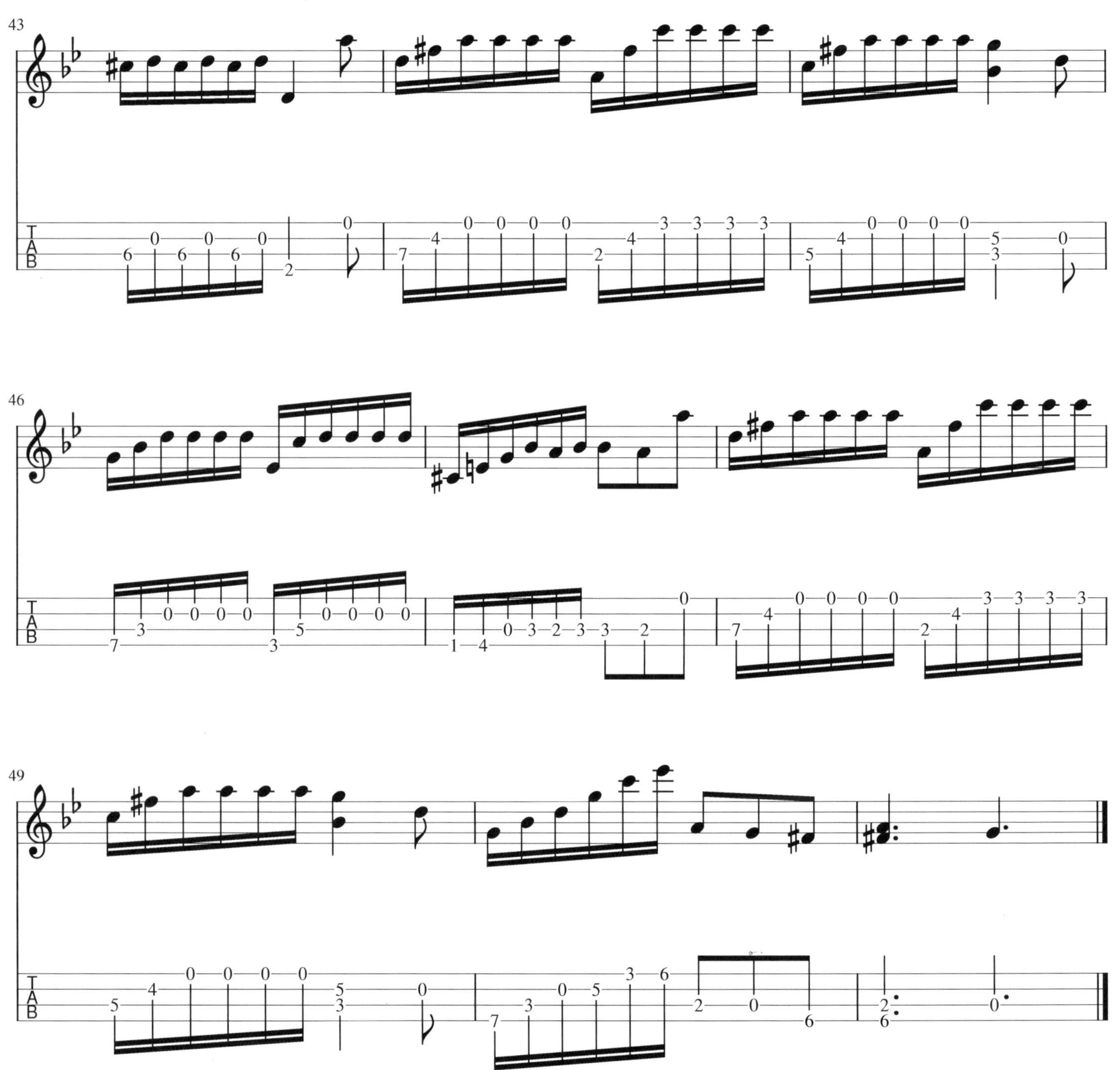
43
46
49

This page has been left blank to avoid an awkward page turn.

Alemanda

Arranged by
Rob MacKillop

Libro per la Mandola, 1703

Niccolo Ceccherini

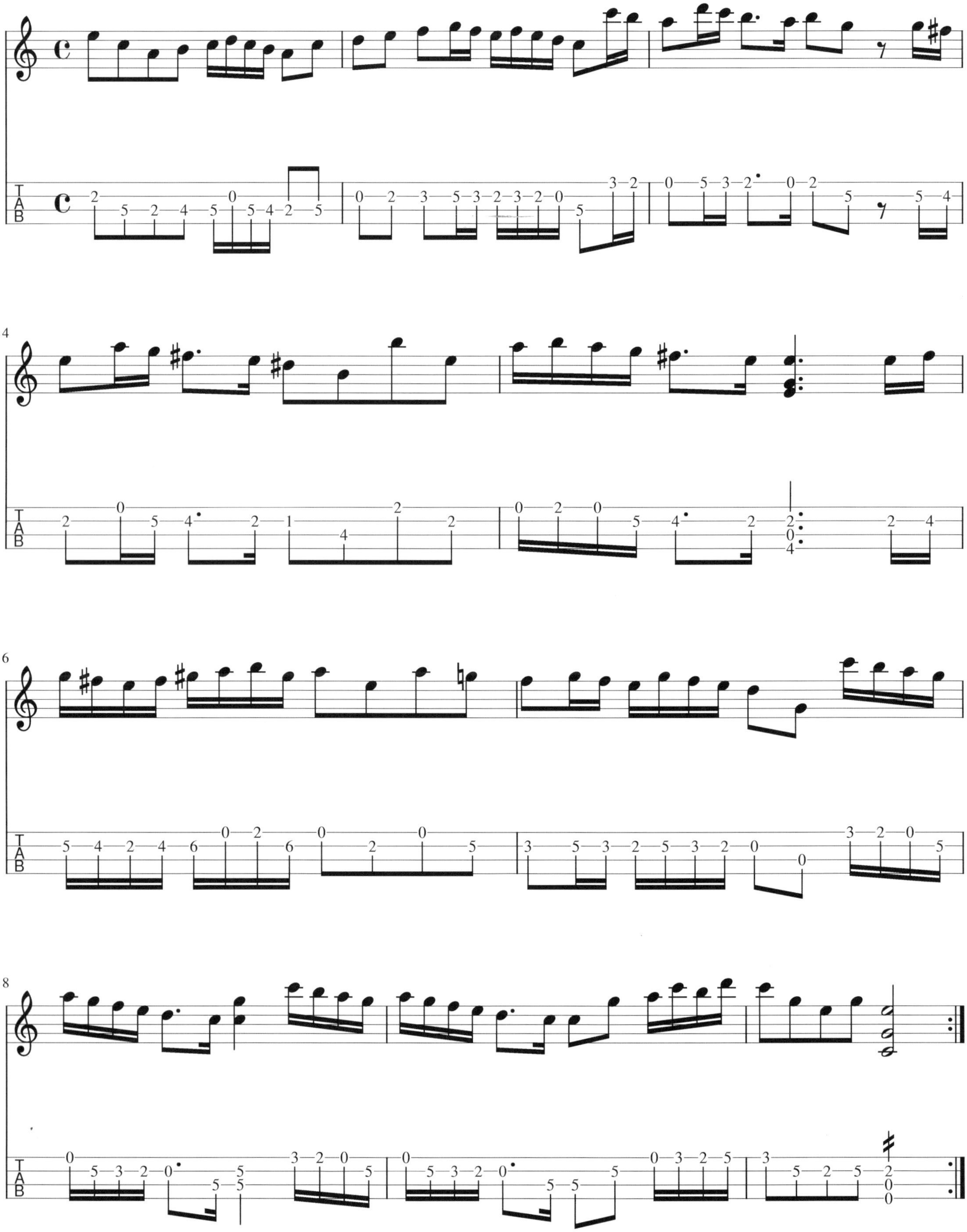

4

6

8

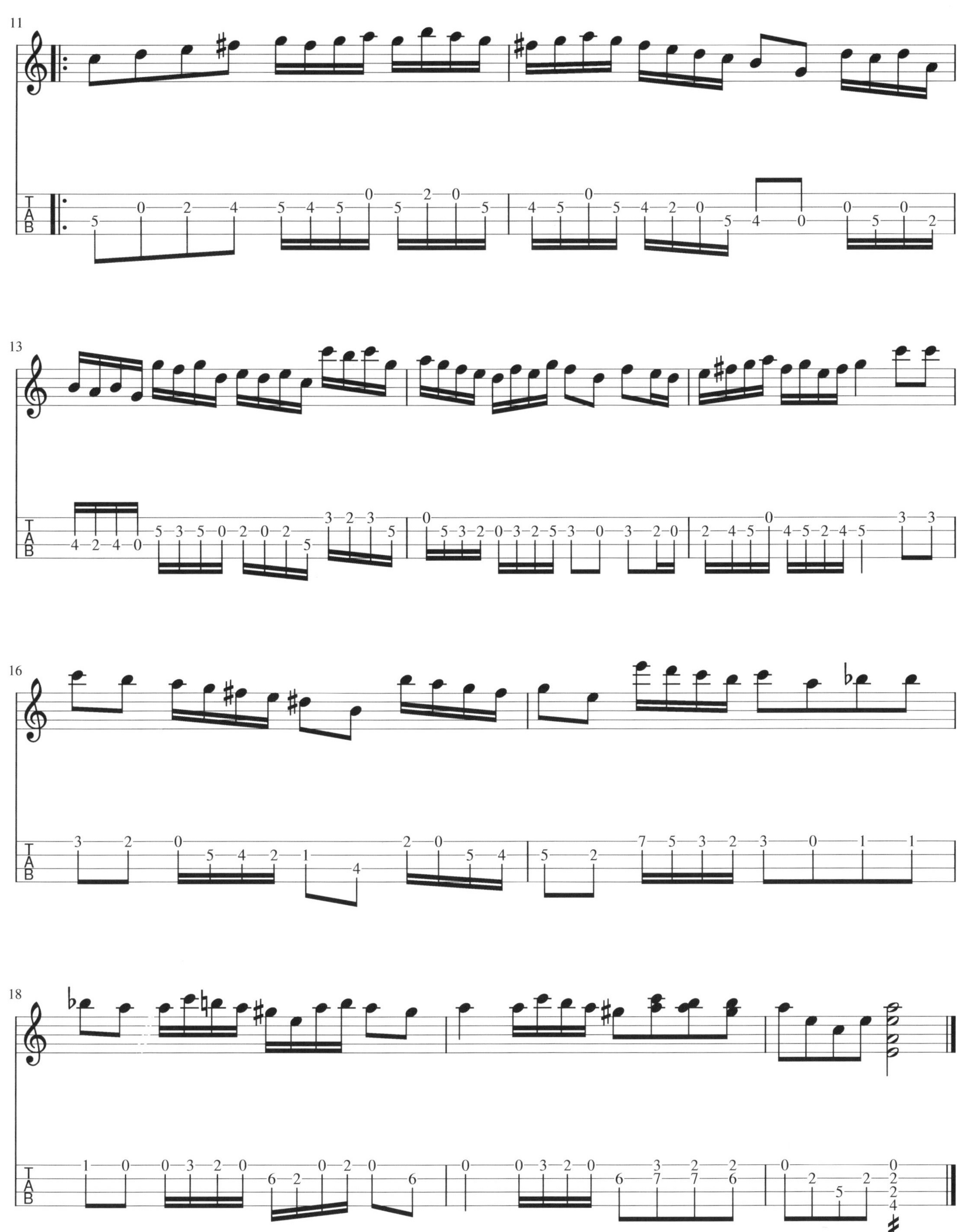
11
TAB
13
TAB
16
TAB
18
TAB

Fuga

Arranged by
Rob MacKillop

Libro per la Mandola, 1703

Niccolo Ceccherini

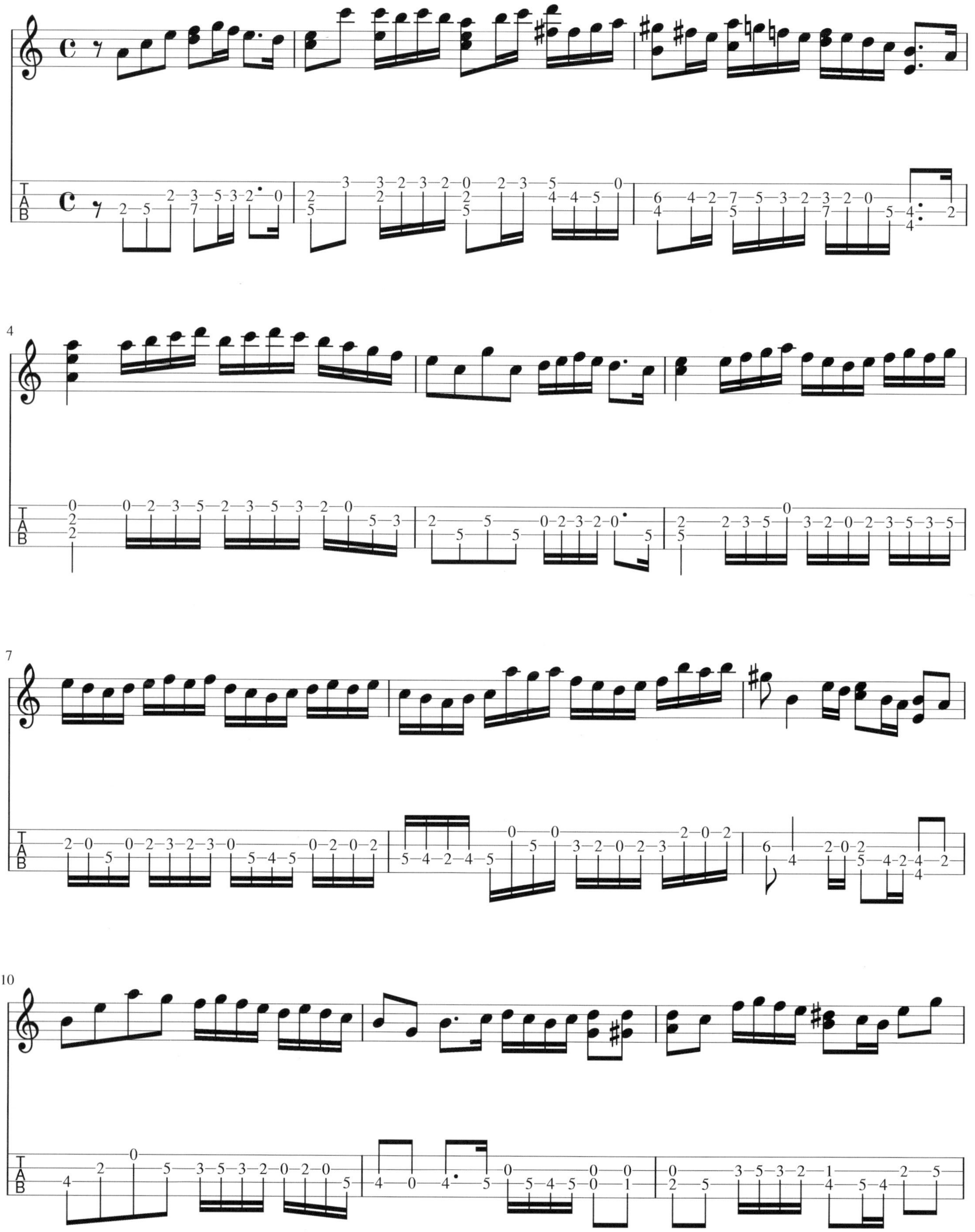

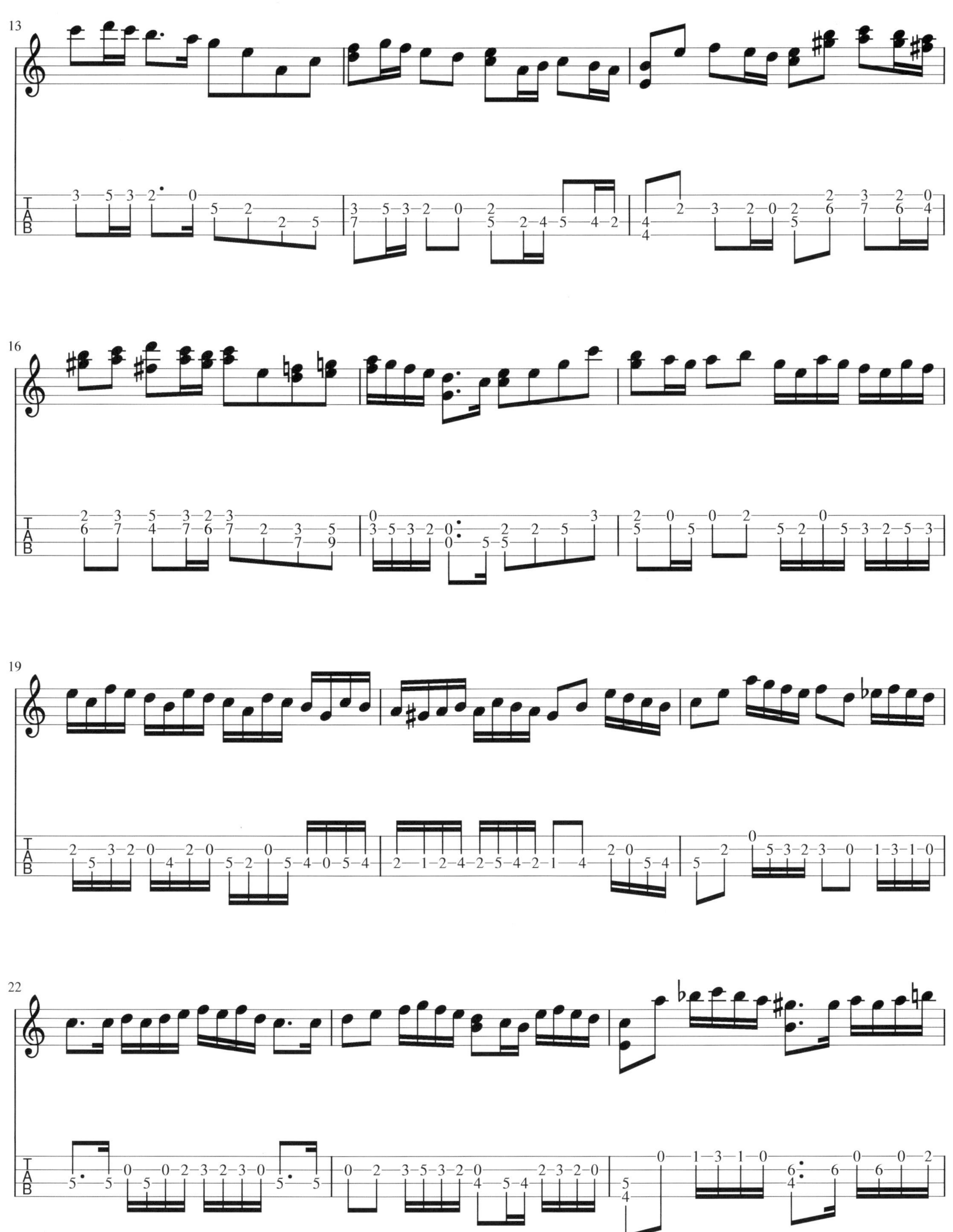
13
16
19
22

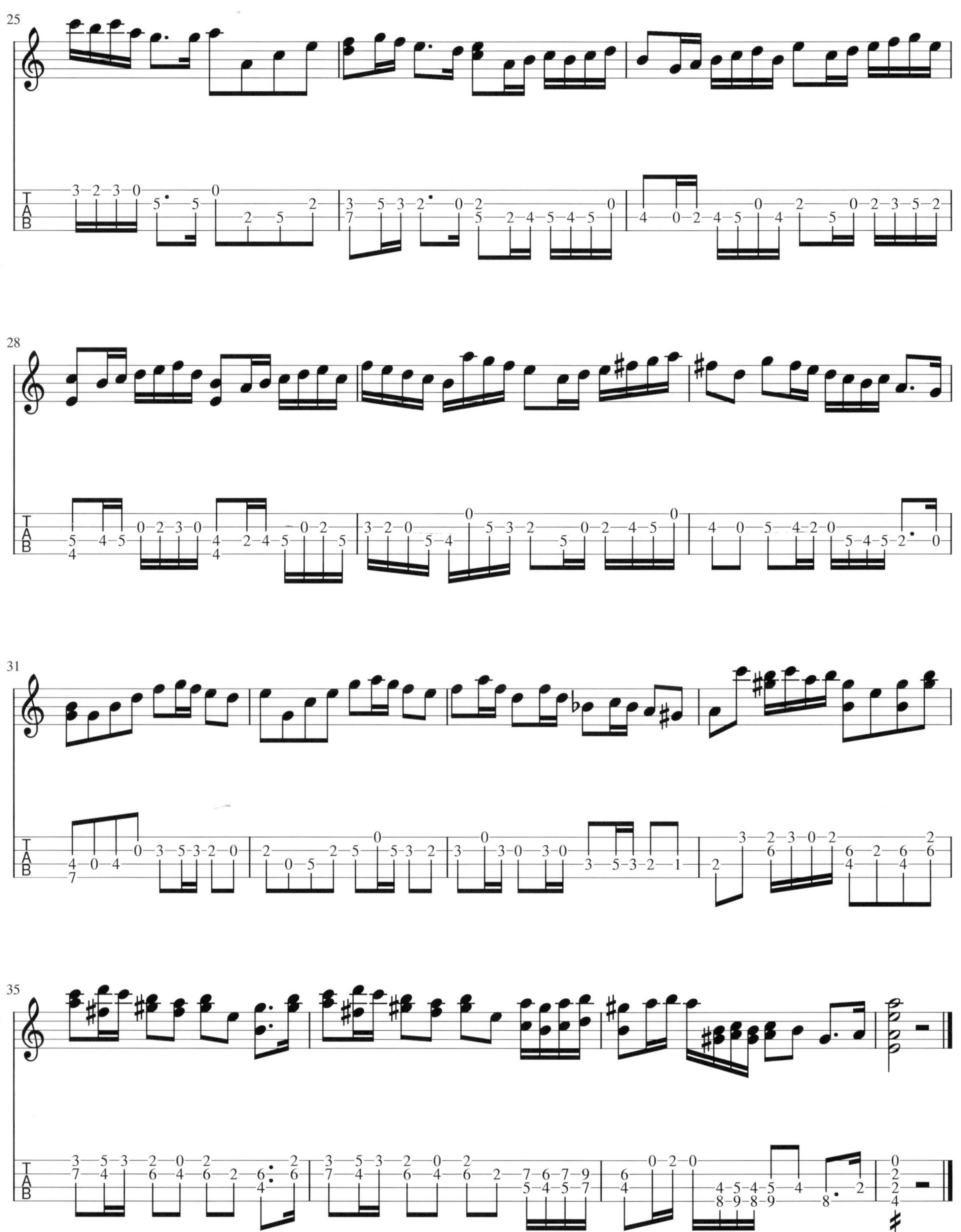

This page has been left blank to avoid an awkward page turn.

Arpeggio Example 1

Arranged by
Rob MacKillop

Essai 1824, p. 83

J. L. Duport

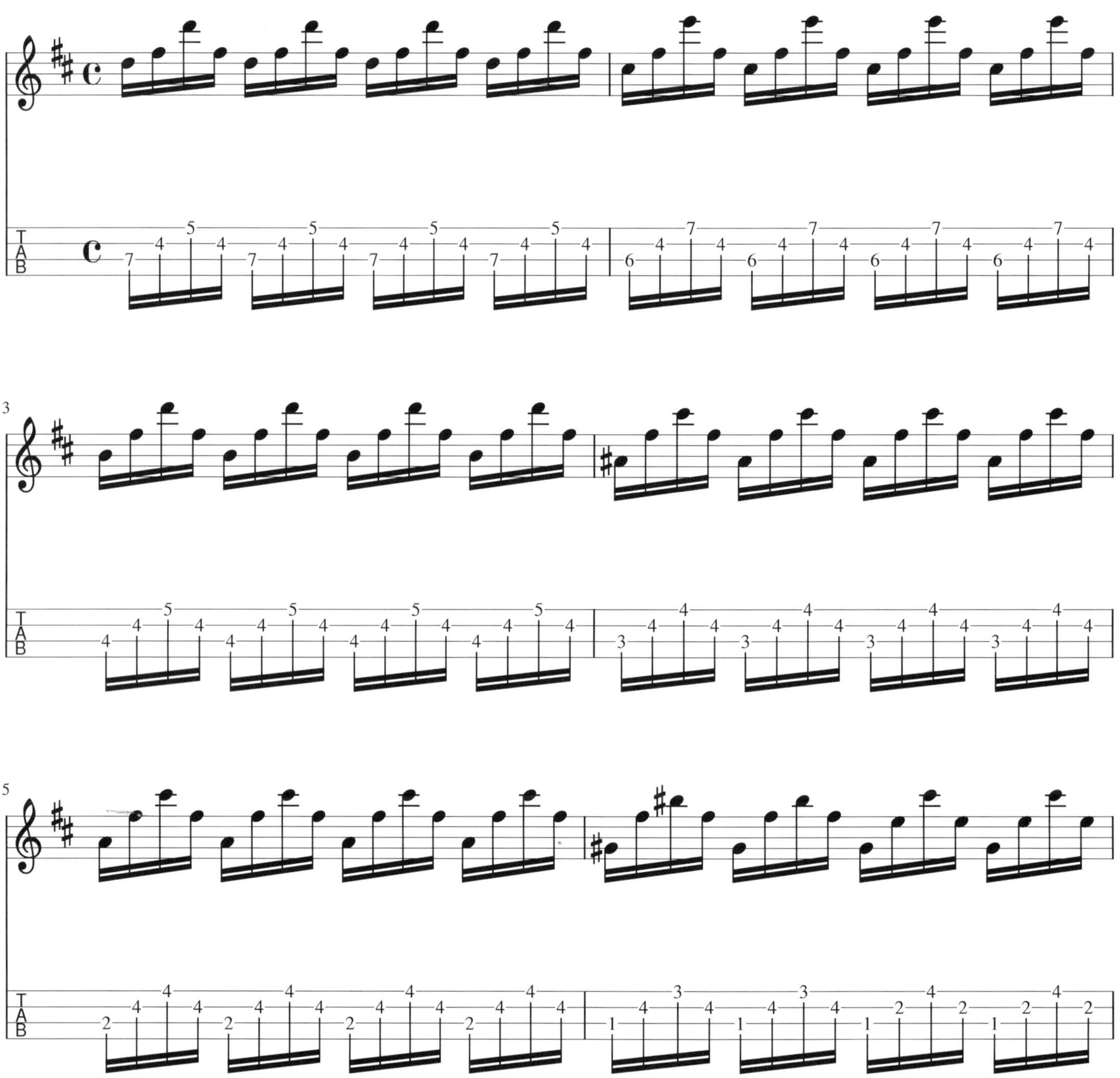

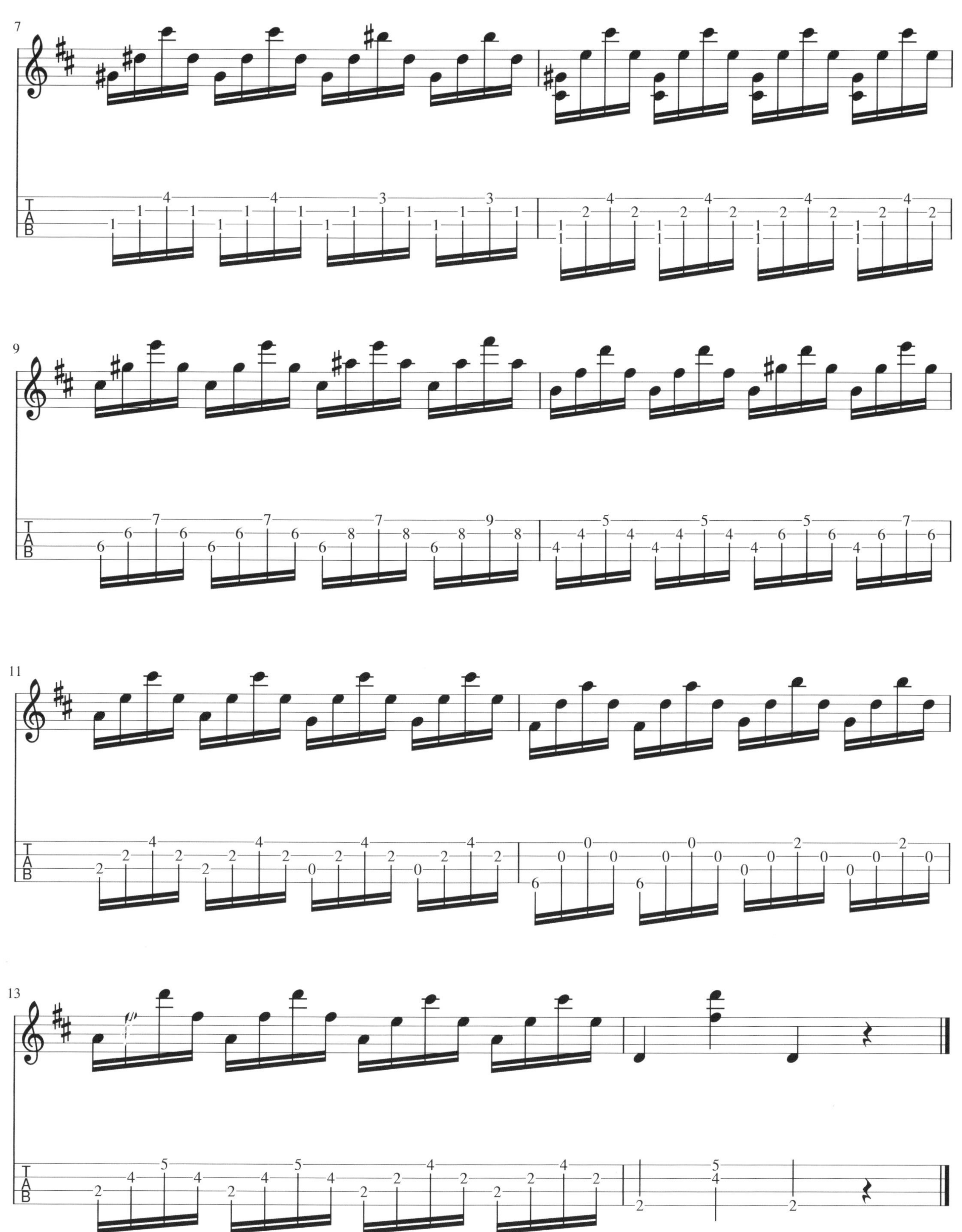
7
T
A
B
9
11
13

Arranged by
Rob MacKillop

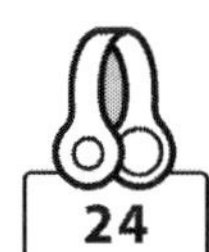

Arpeggio Example 2

Essai 1824, p. 84

J. L. Duport

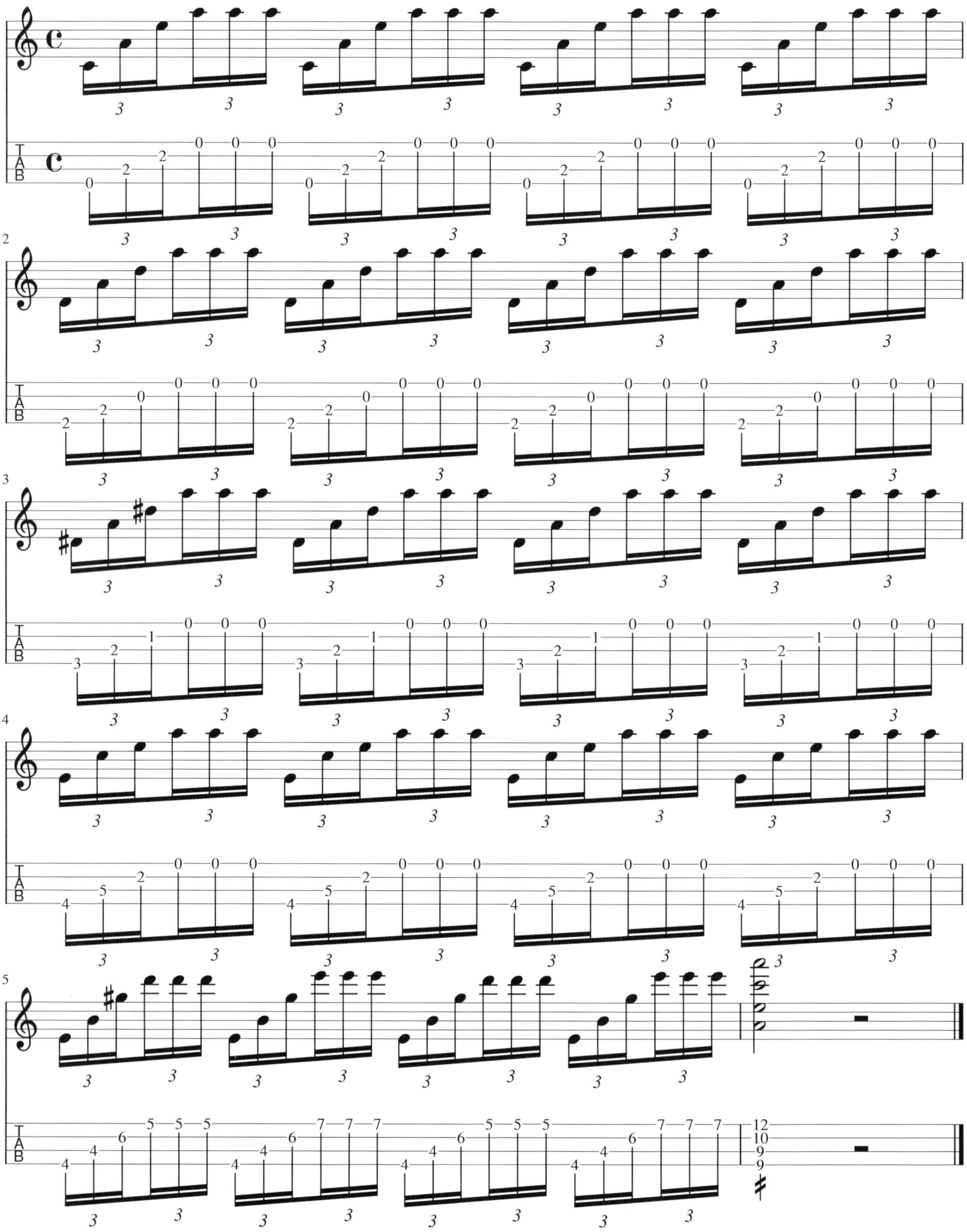

This page has been left blank to avoid an awkward page turn.

Arranged by
Rob MacKillop

25

Chromatic Passage in Dm

Essai 1824, p. 101

J. L. Duport

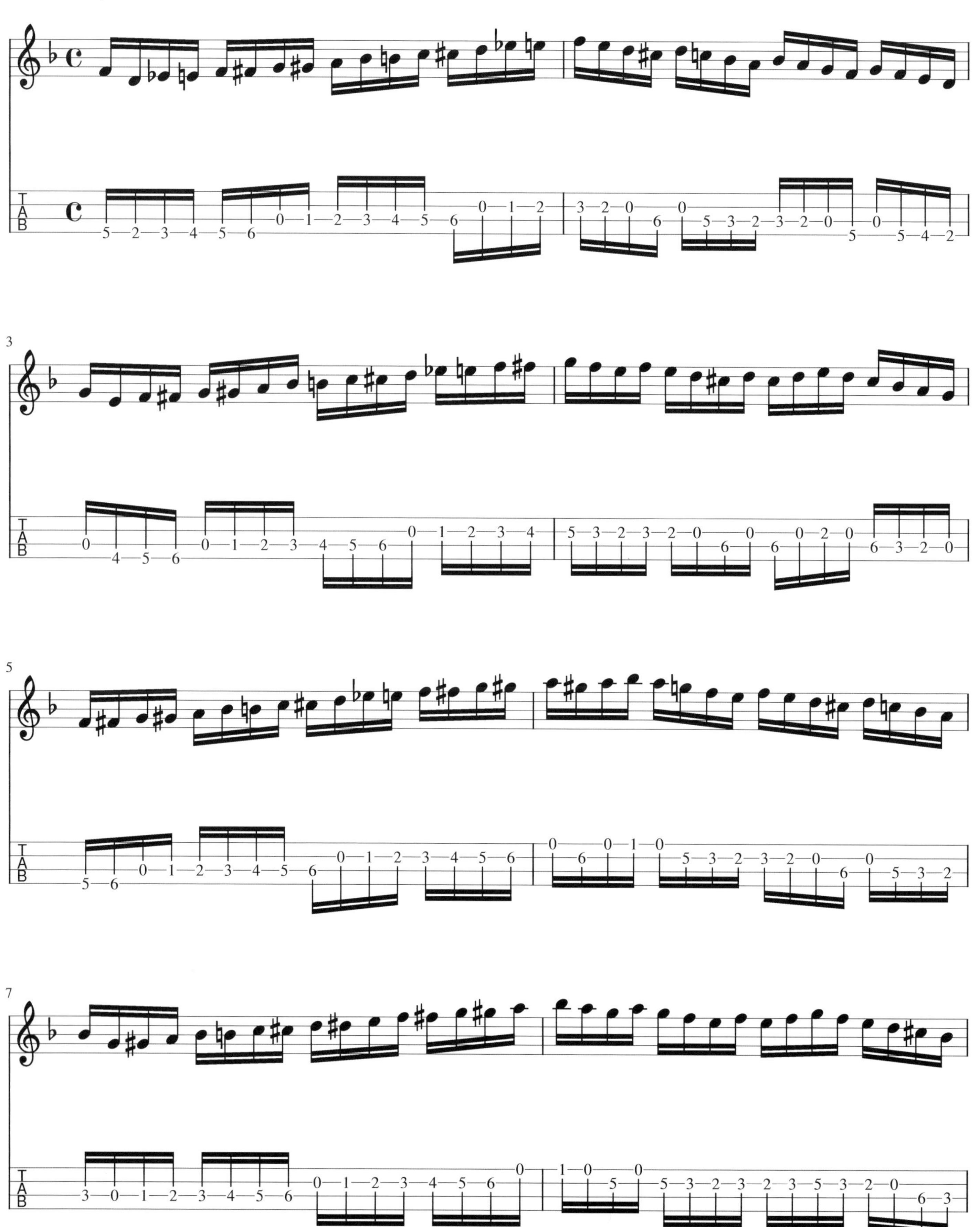

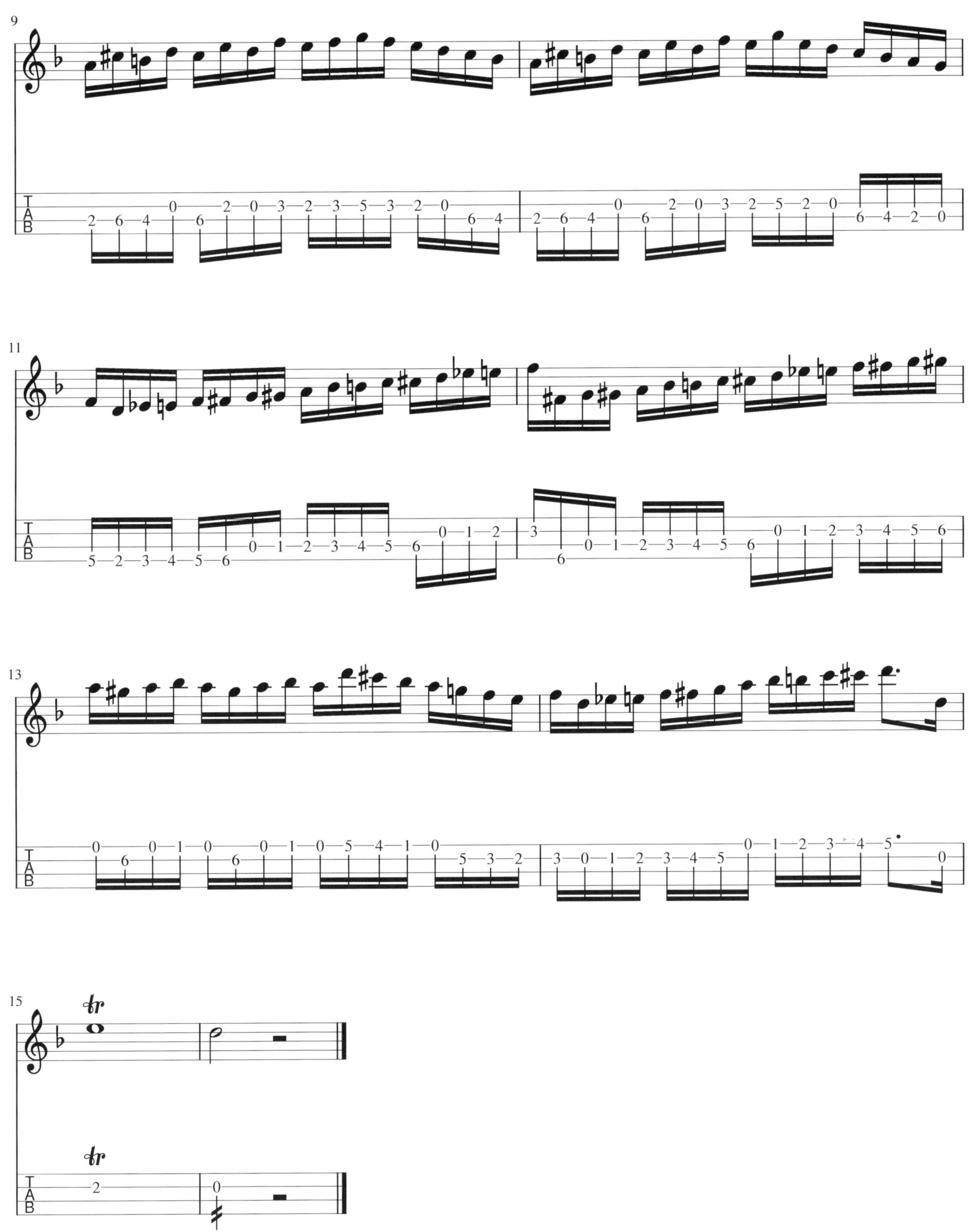
9
11
13
15
tr
TAB

Passage in F Major

Arranged by
Rob MacKillop

Essai 1824, p. 111

J. L. Duport

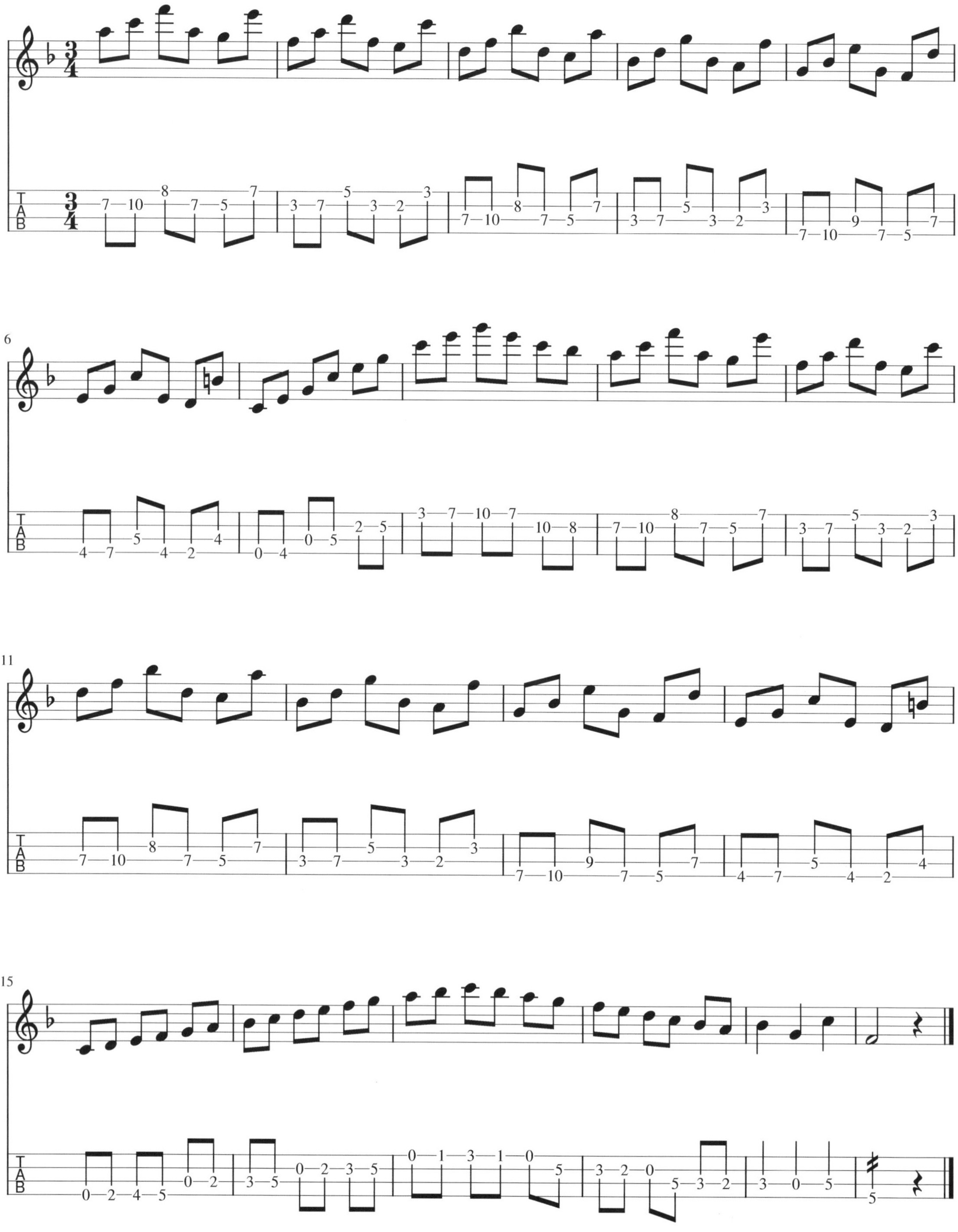

Op. 60 No. 3

Arranged by
Rob MacKillop

Introduction to the Study
of the Guitar, 1837

F. Sor

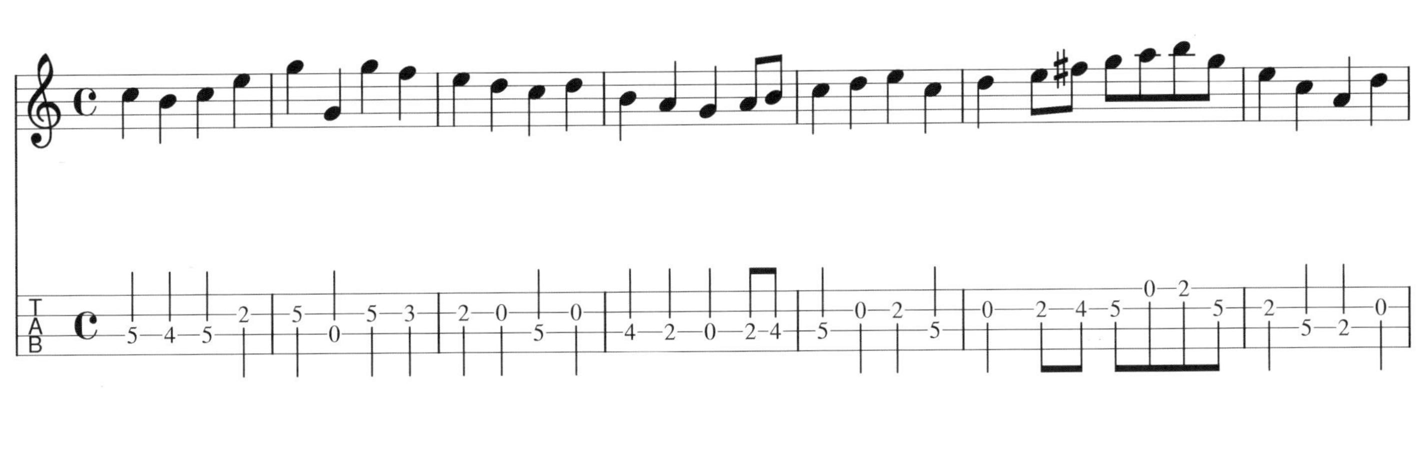

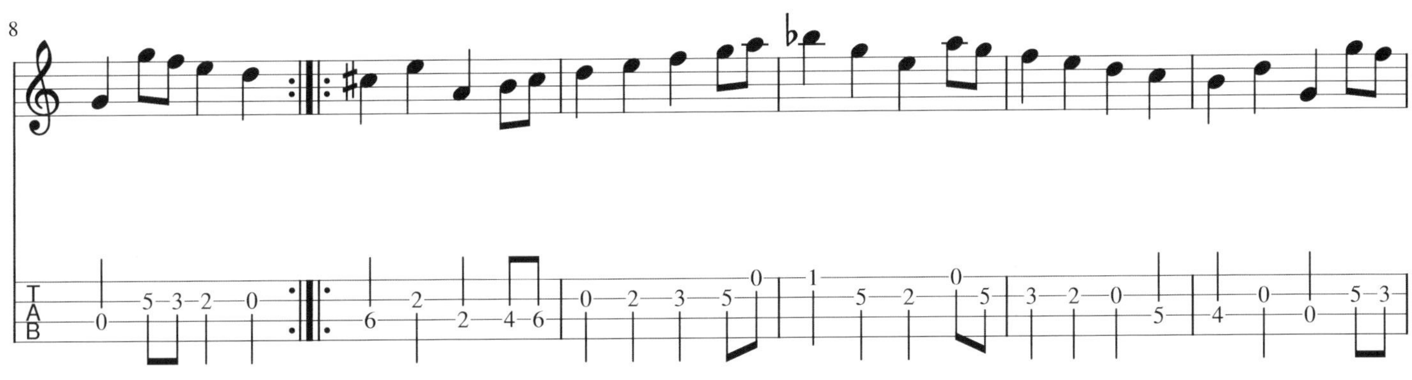

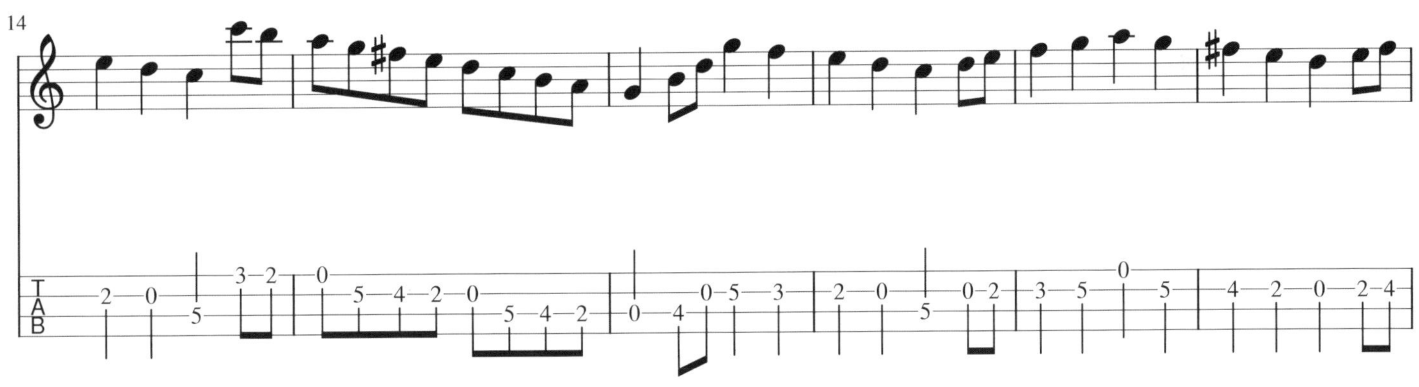

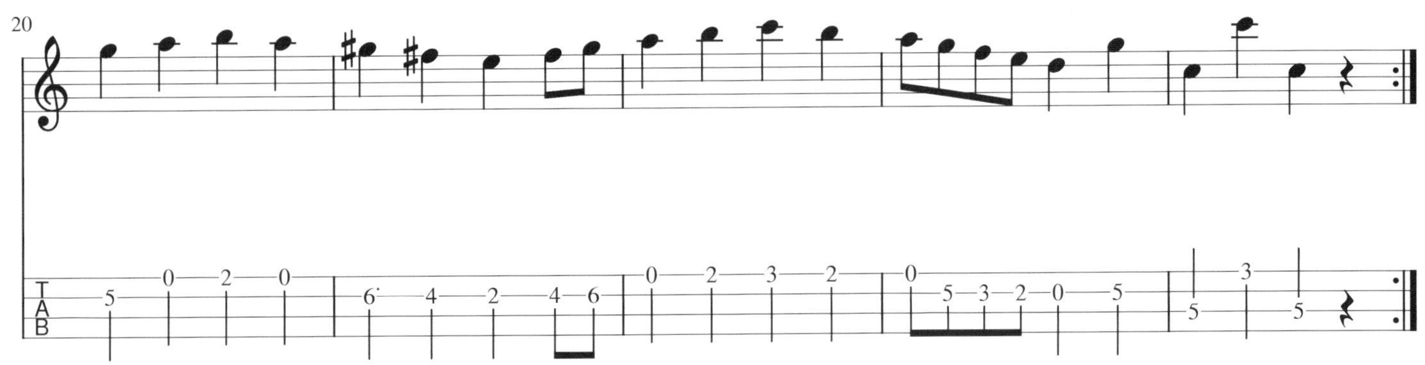

Op. 60 No. 4

Arranged by
Rob MacKillop

Introduction to the Study
of the Guitar, 1837

F. Sor

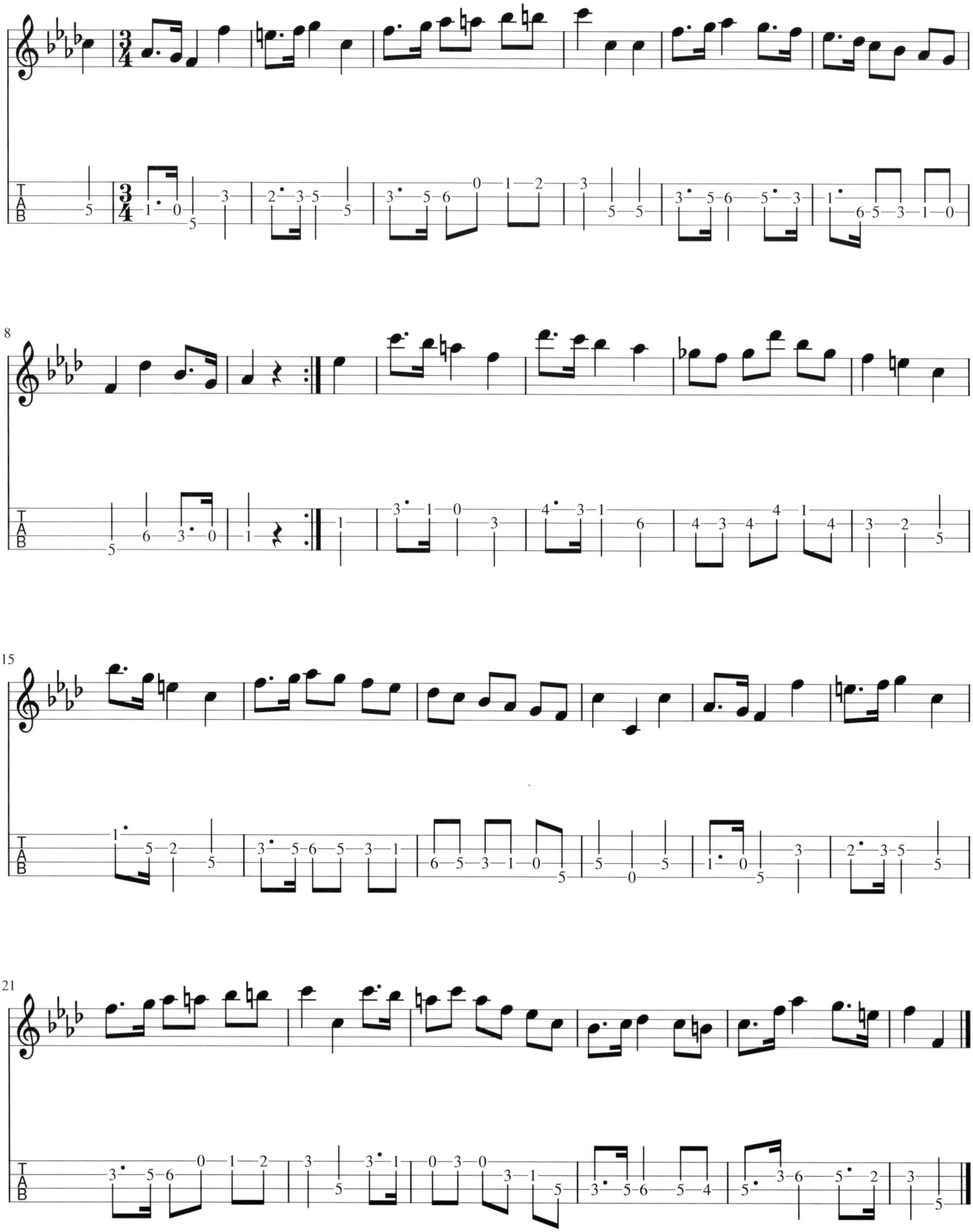

This page has been left blank to avoid an awkward page turn.

Op. 76a No. 1

Arranged by
Rob MacKillop

29

Fünfzehn leichte melodisch-rhythmische Etüden

D. Popper

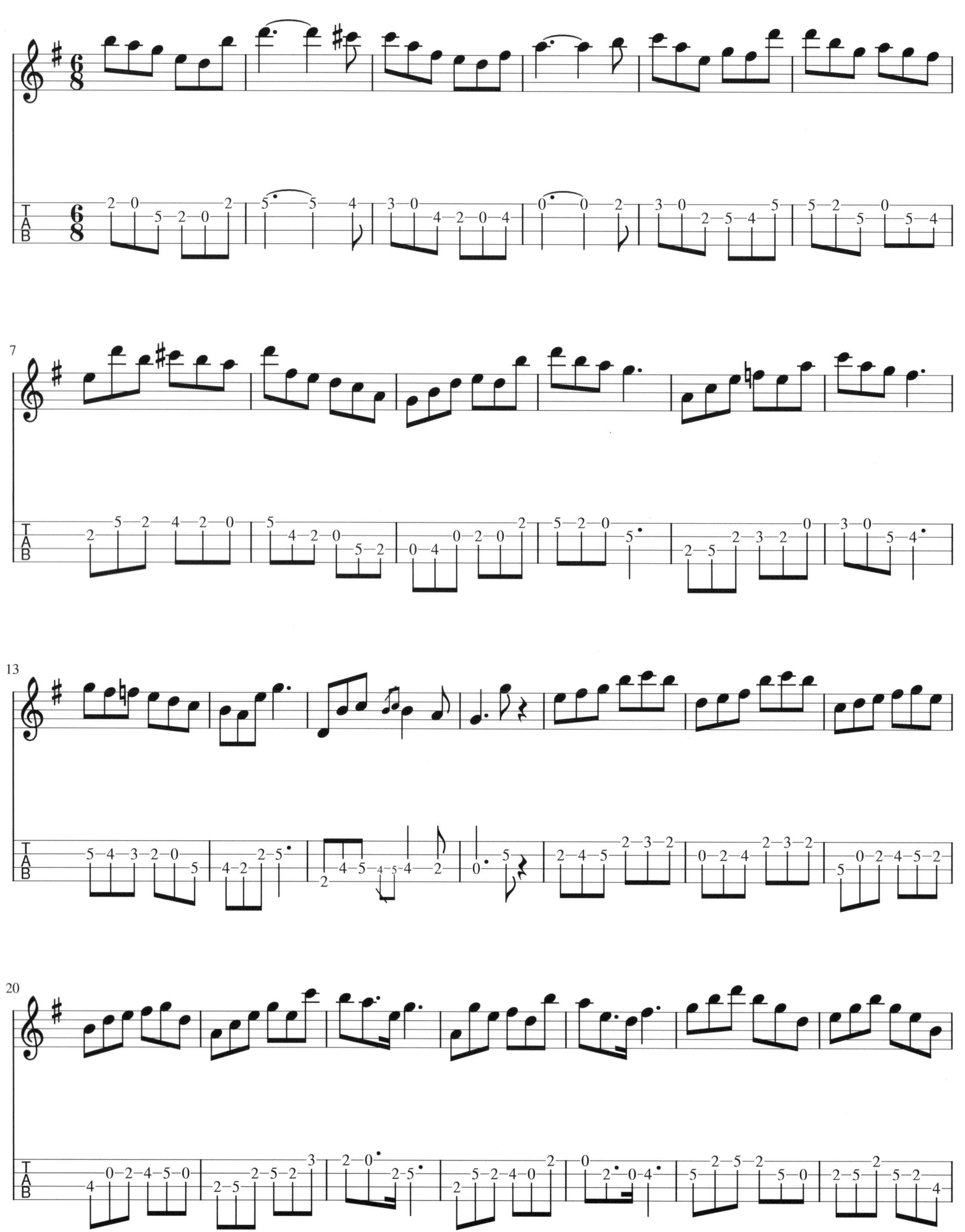

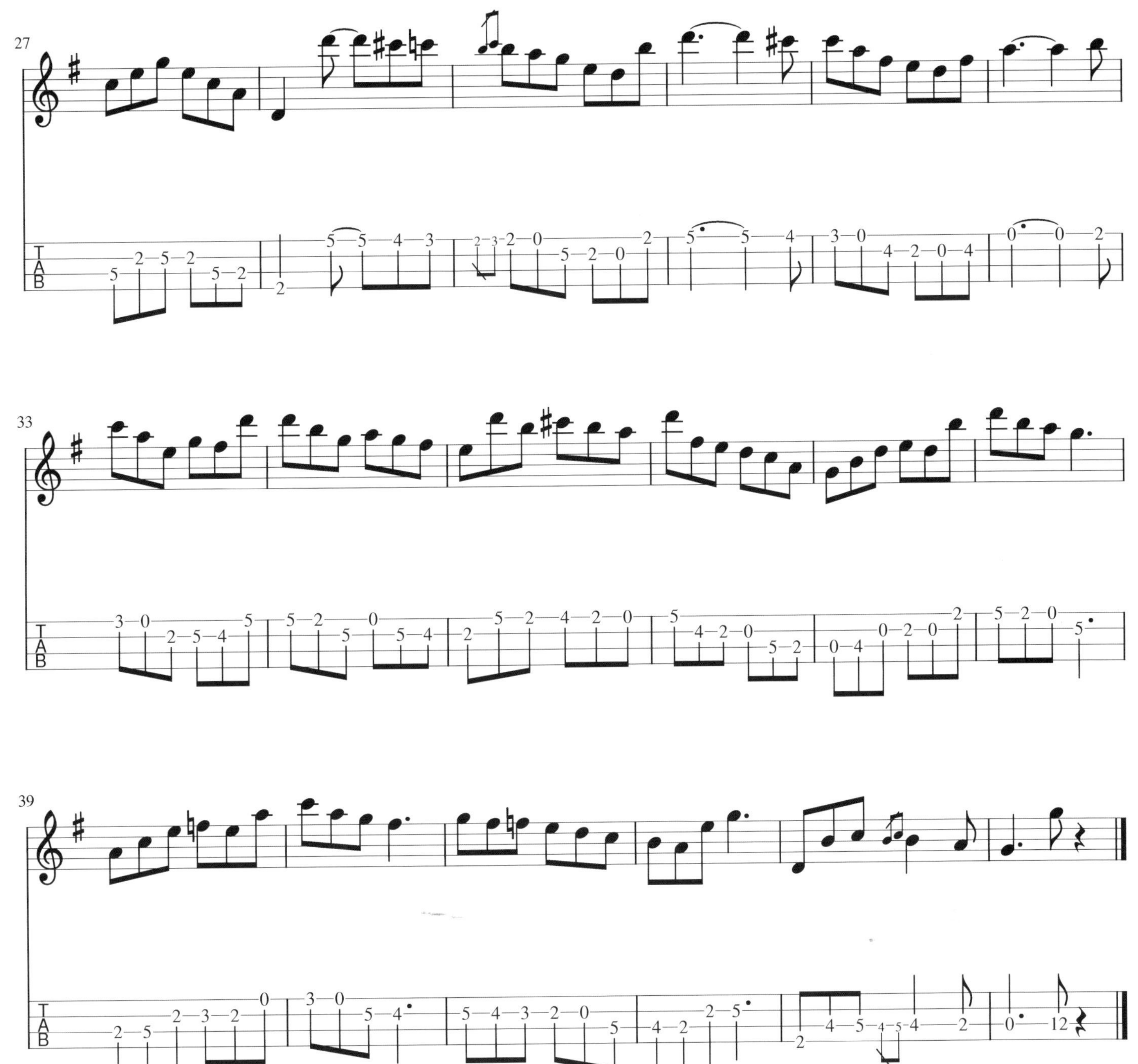

Op. 76a No. 2

Arranged by
Rob MacKillop

30

Fünfzehn leichte melodisch-rhythmische Etüden

D. Popper

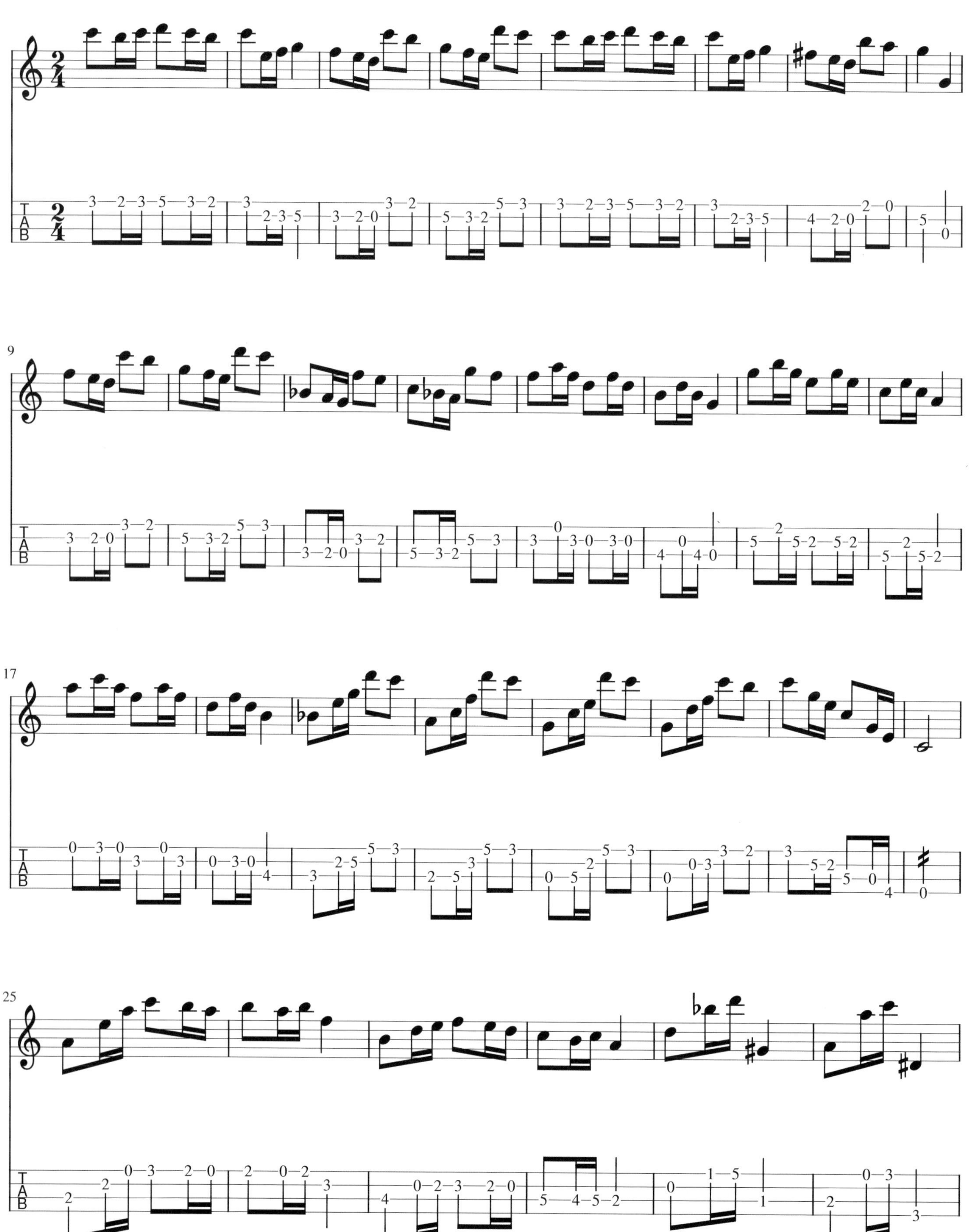

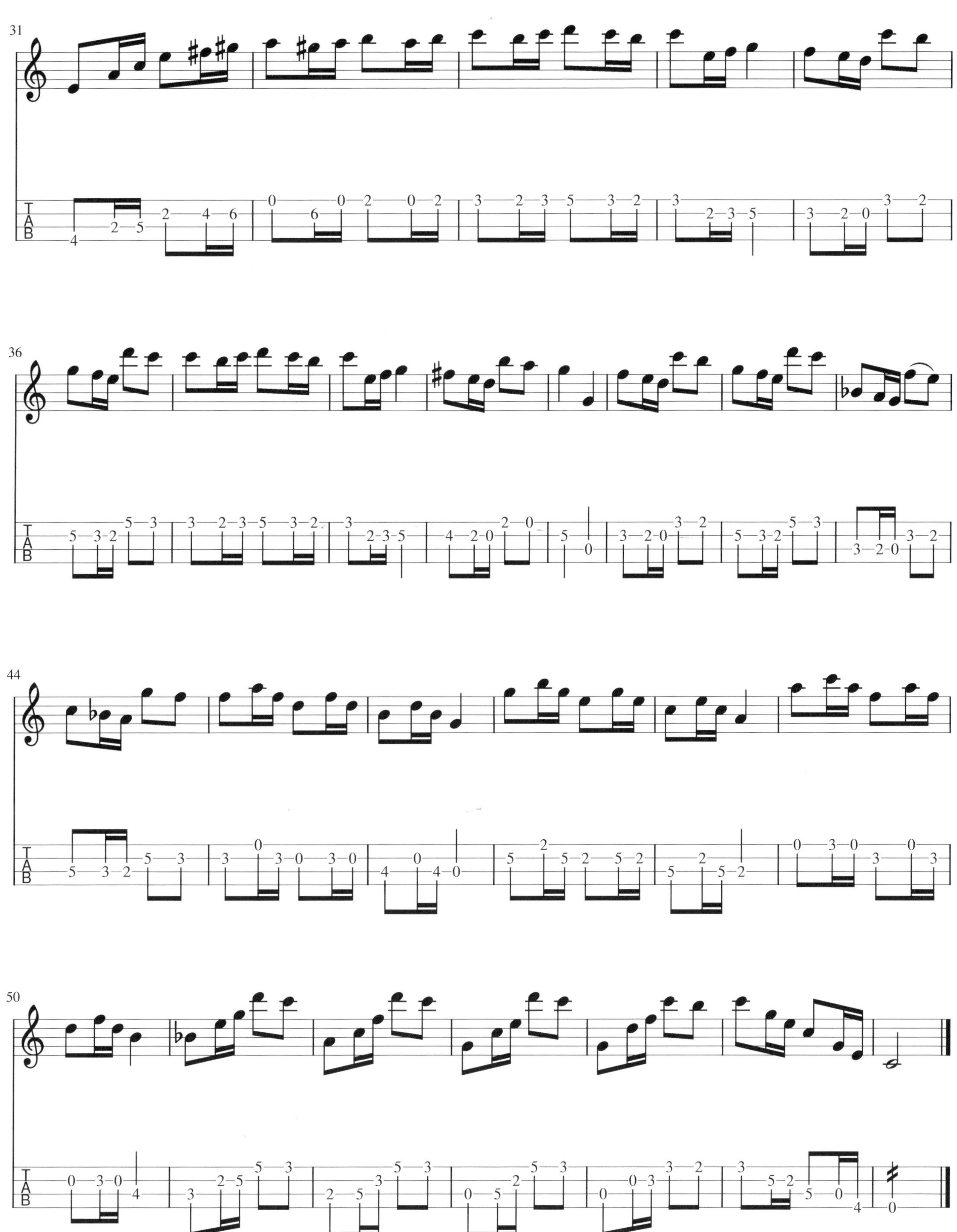
31
36
44
50

Op. 76a No. 3

Arranged by
Rob MacKillop

31

Fünfzehn leichte melodisch-rhythmische Etüden

D. Popper

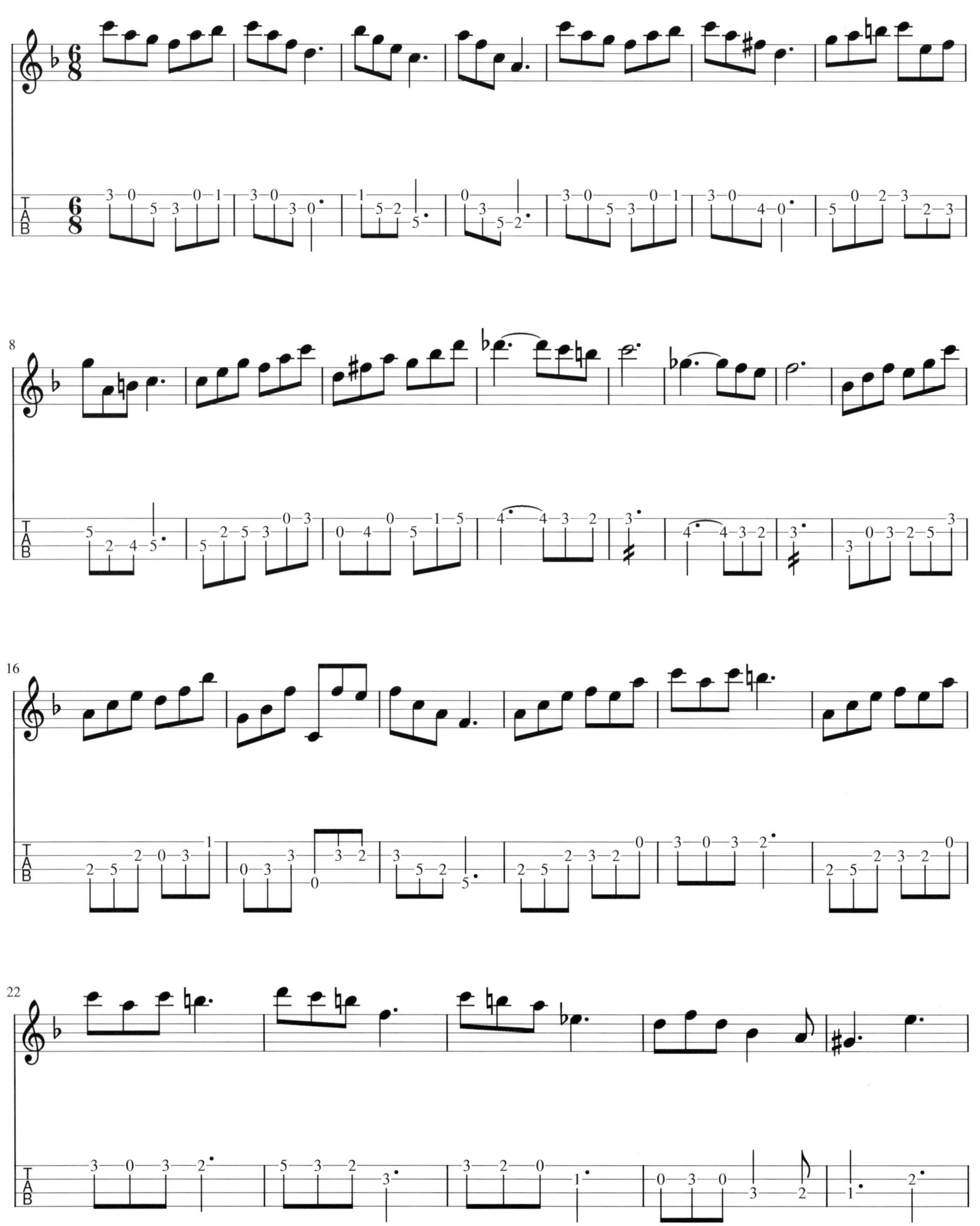

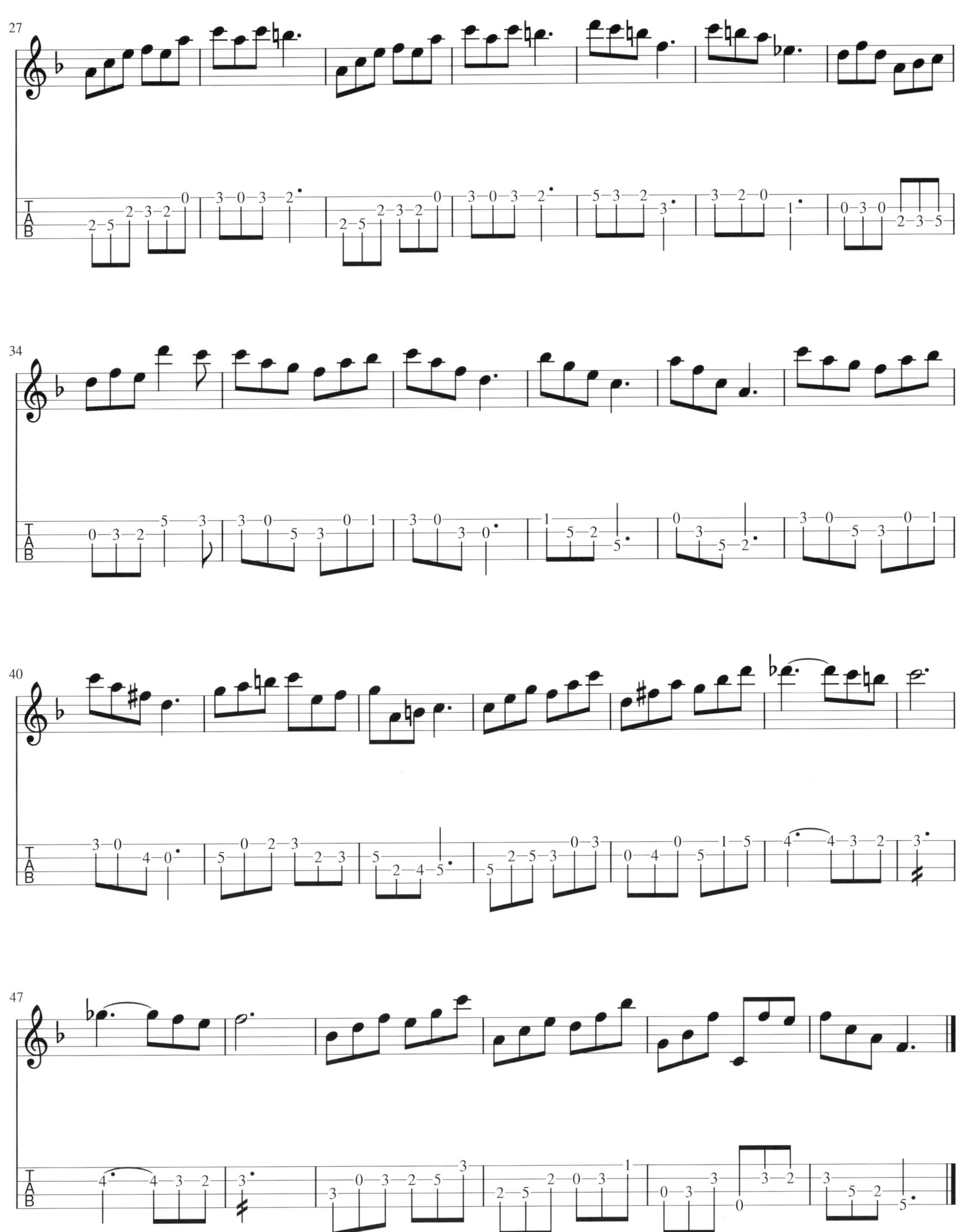
27
34
40
47

Arranged by
Rob MacKillop

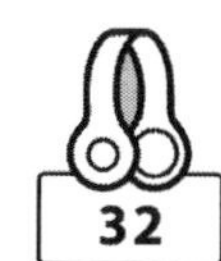

Andante

Method for the Cello, 1891, Ex.52

C. Fischer

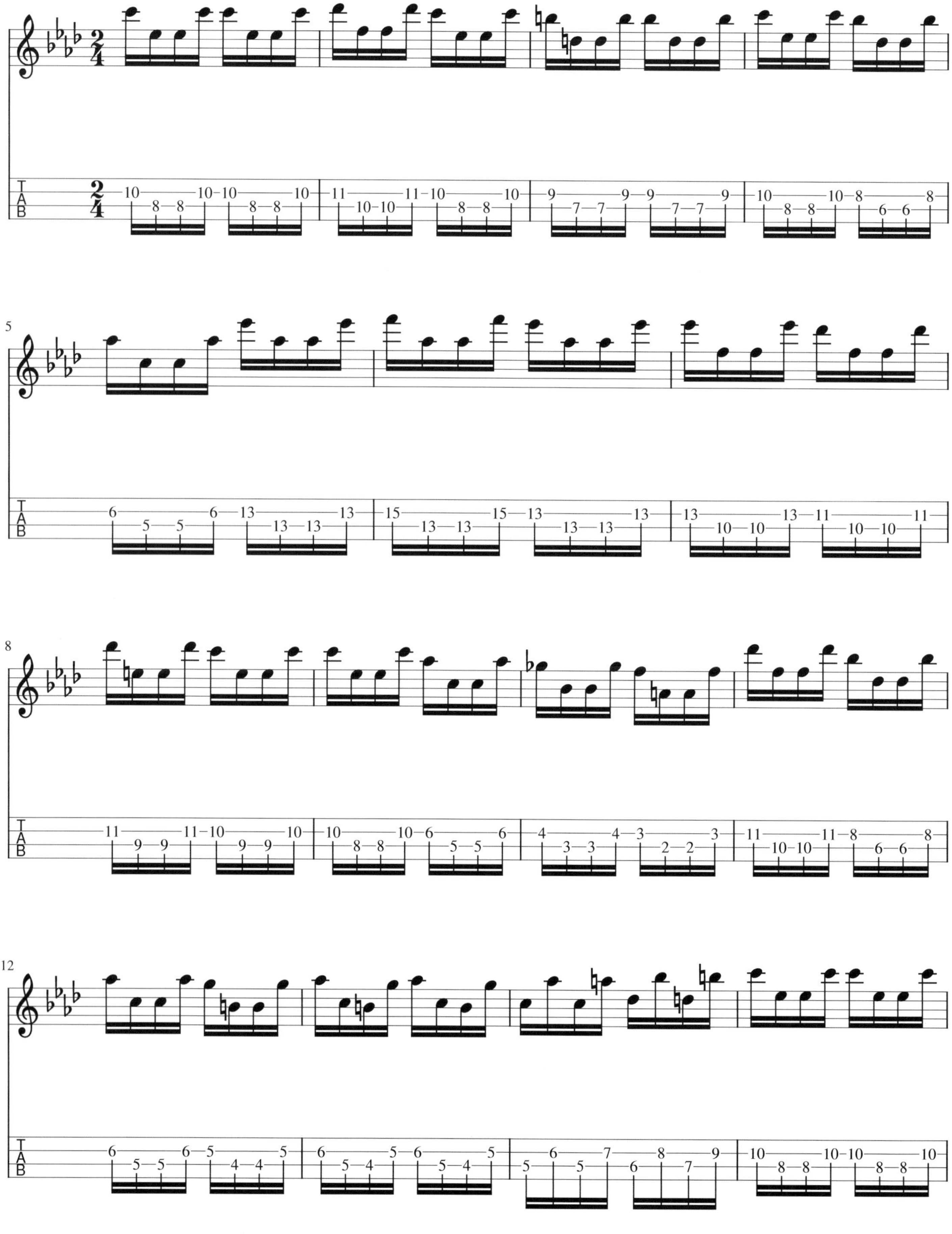

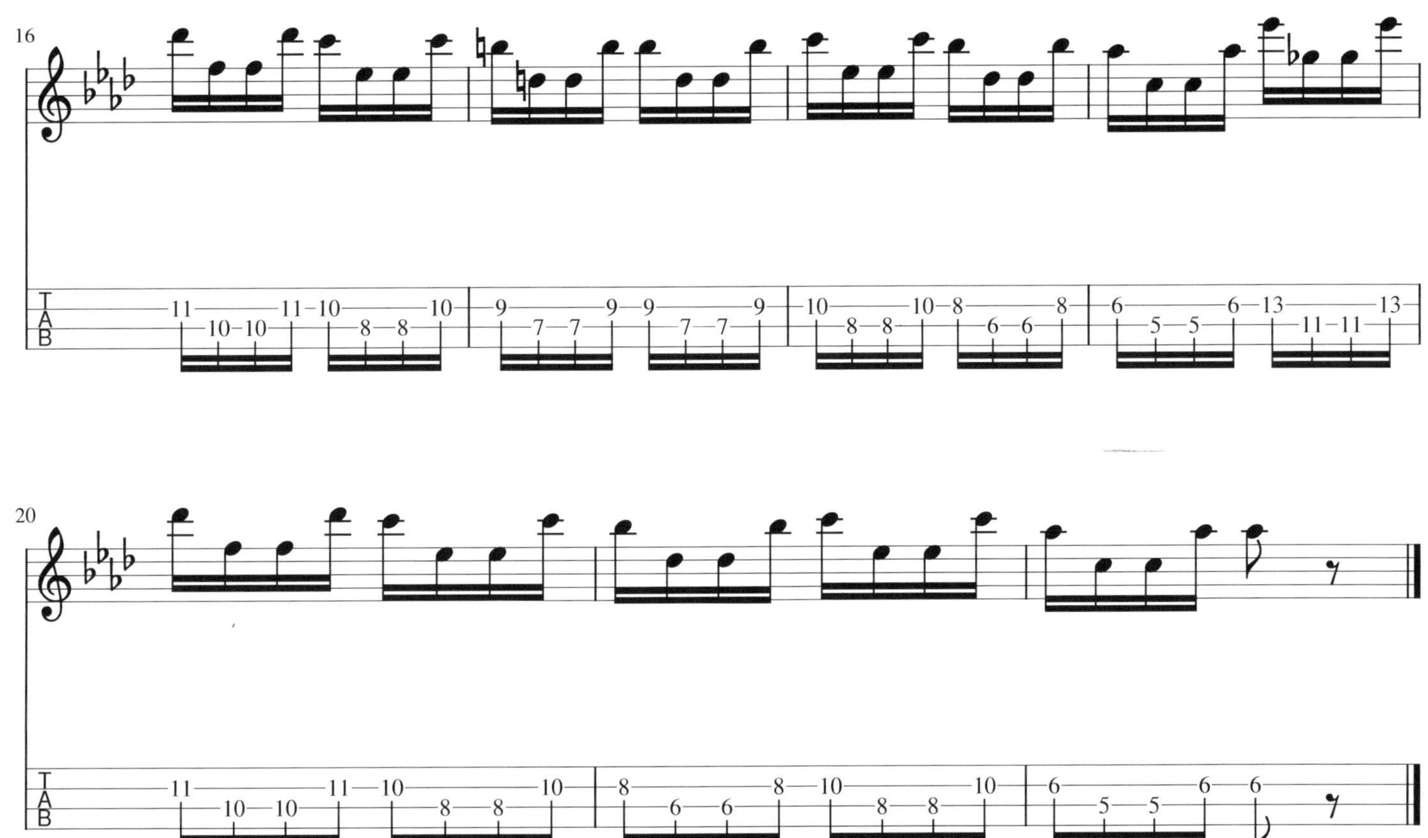
16
TAB
20
TAB

Molto Moderato

Arranged by
Rob MacKillop

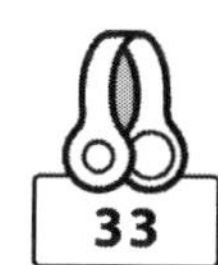

Method for the Cello, 1891, Ex.49

C. Fischer

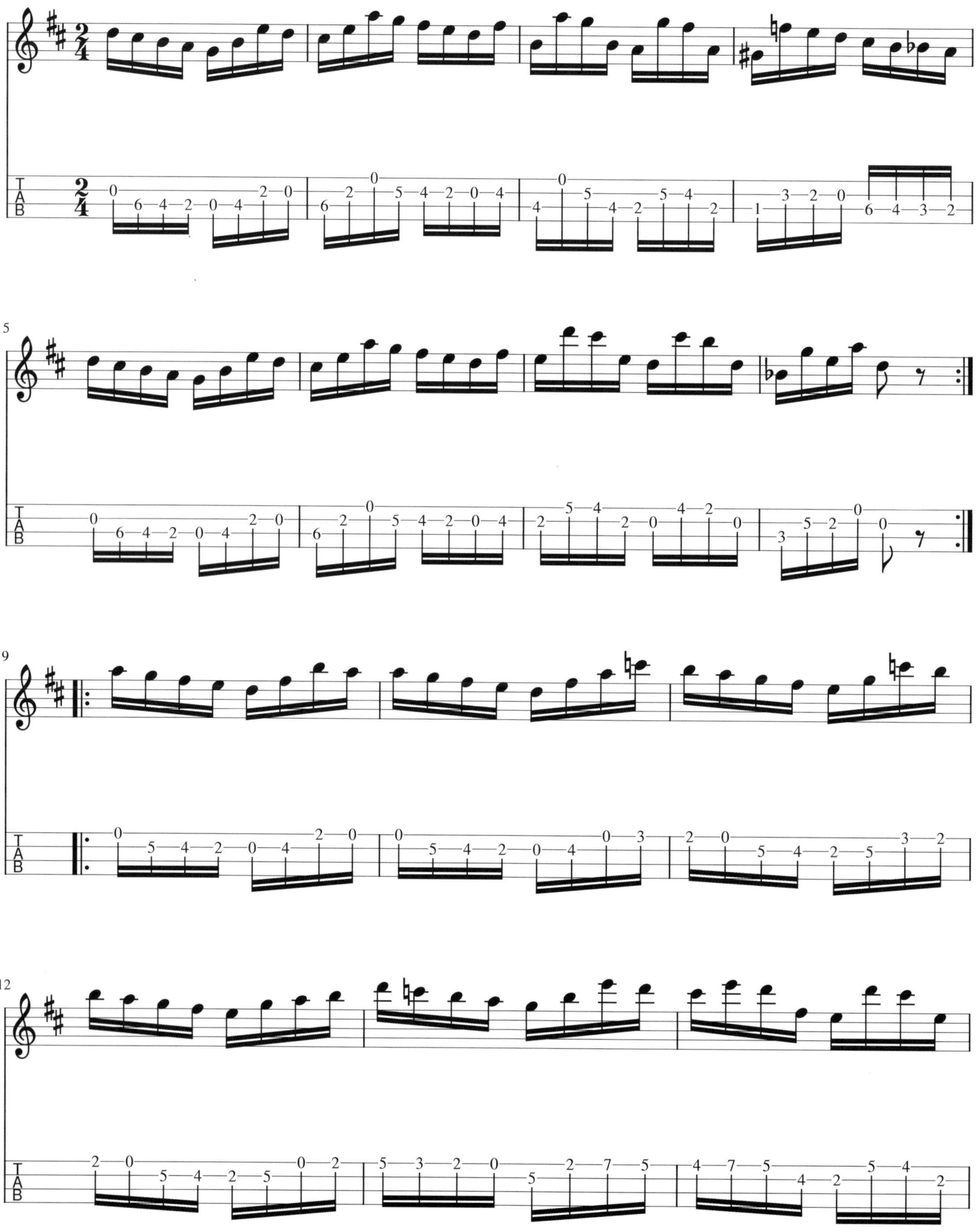

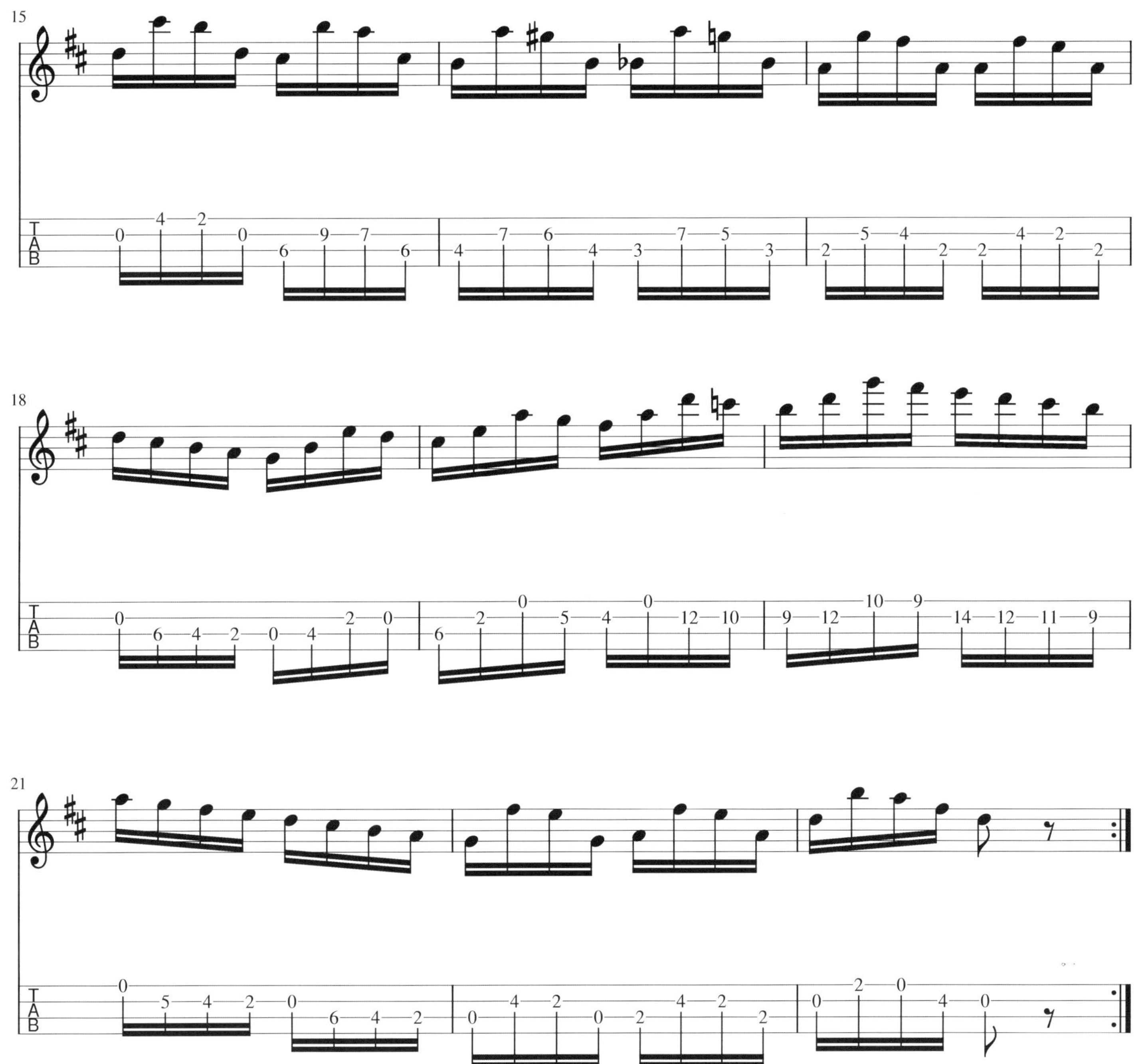

Adagio

Méthode pour Mandoline, No.138

Arranged by
Rob MacKillop

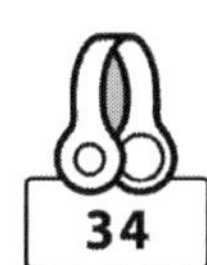

Raffaele Calace

mf

mf

7

f

f

12

p

f
rall.

p

f
rall.

16

p
a tempo

p
a tempo

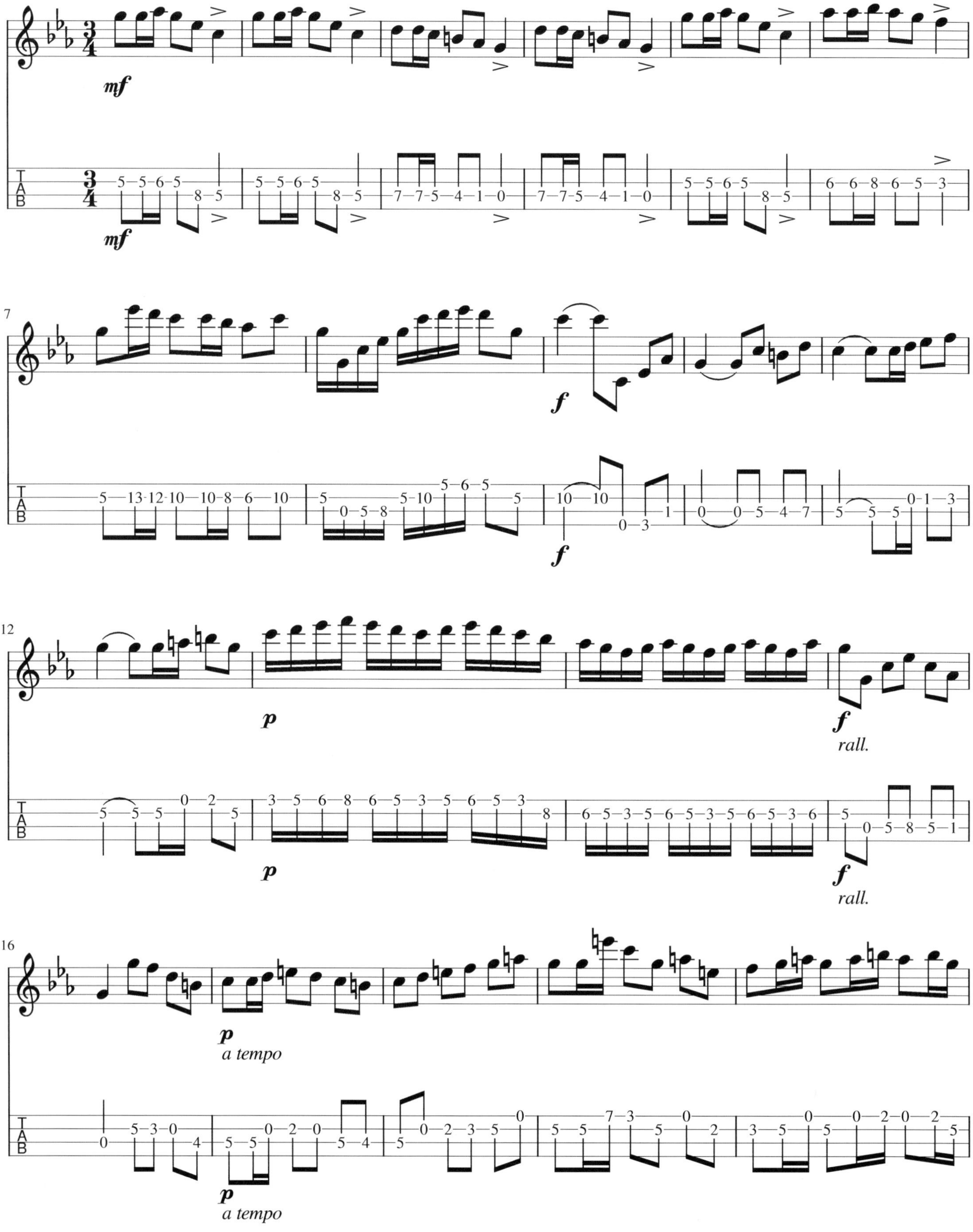

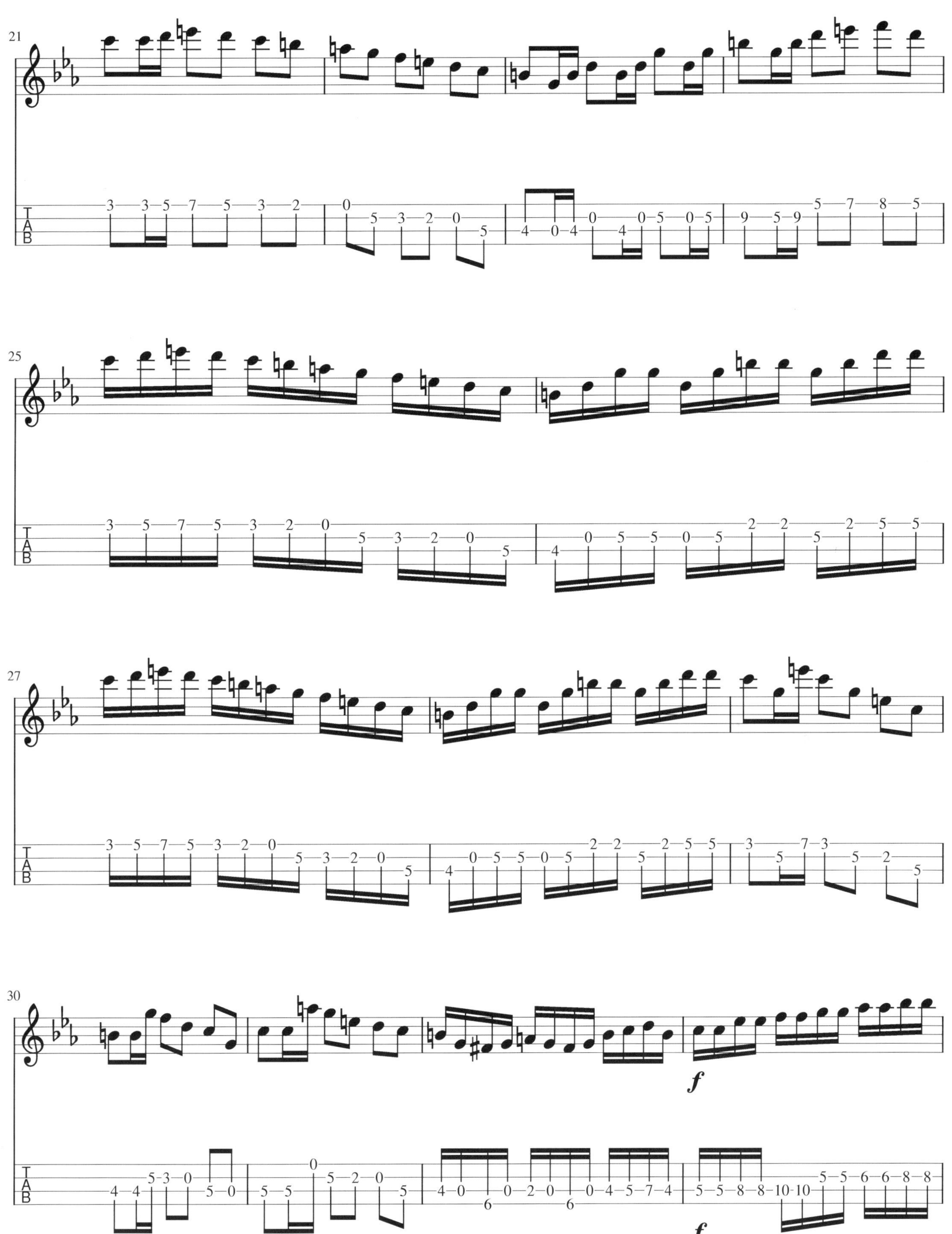
21
25
27
30
f
f

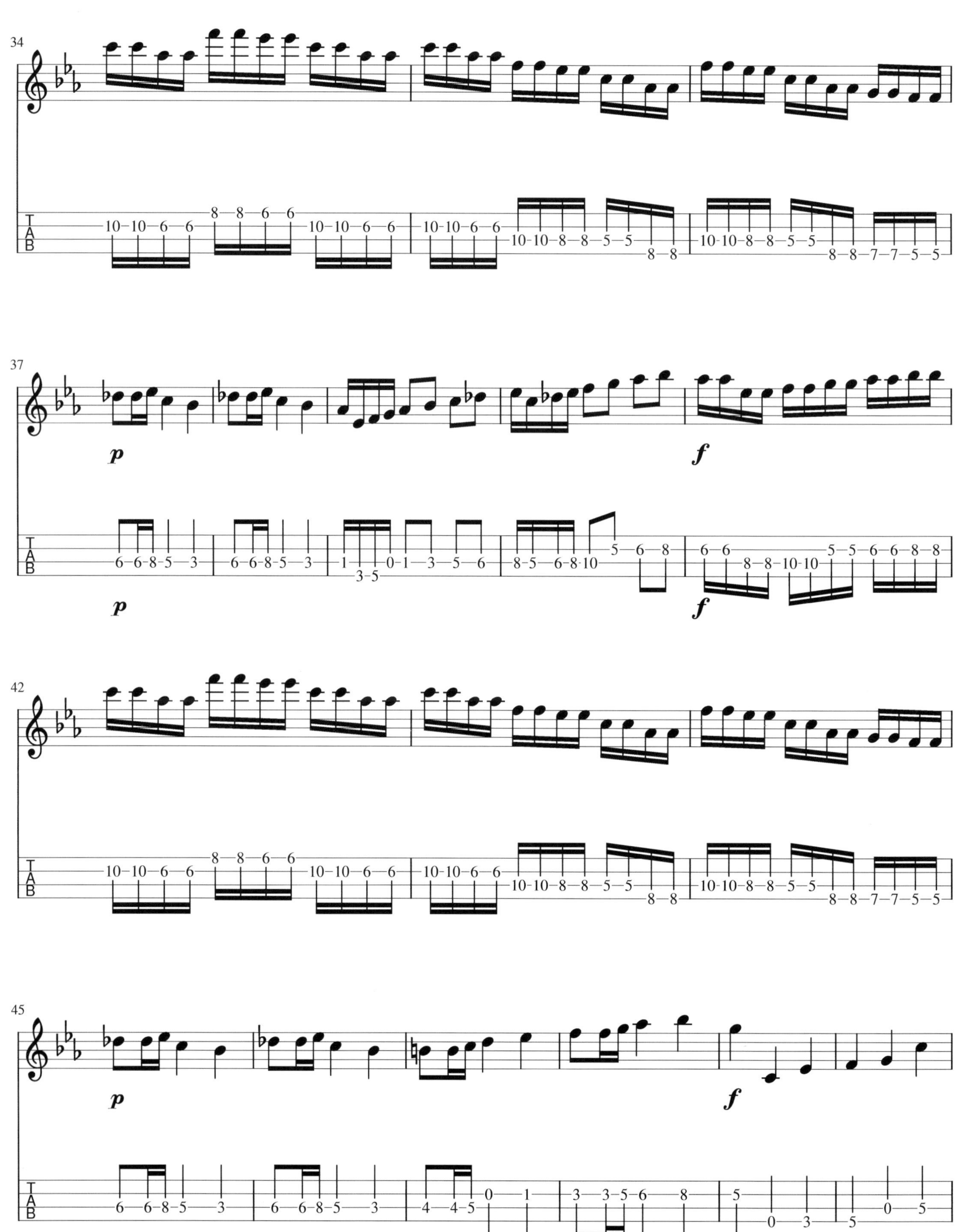
34
37
p
f
42
45
p
f

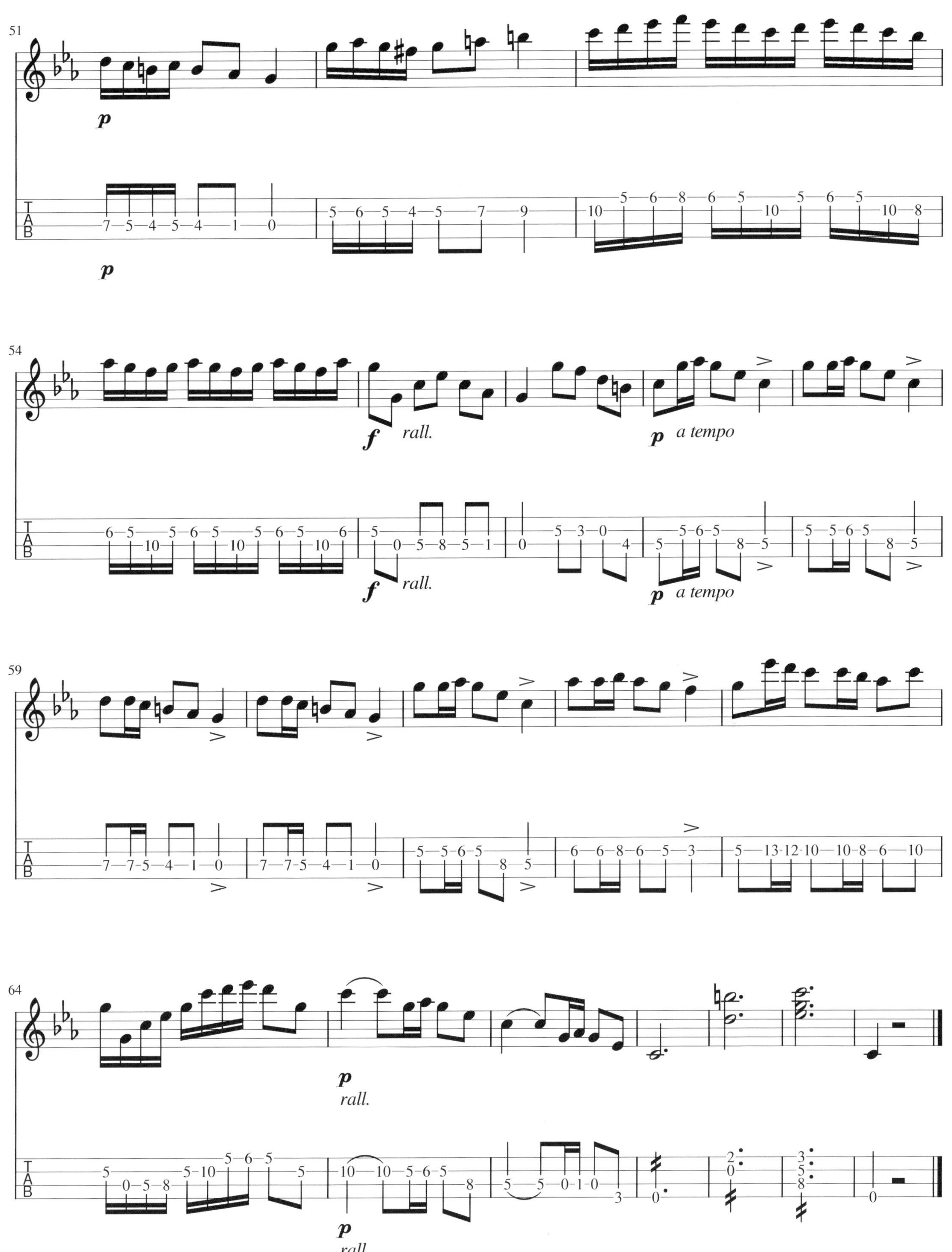
51
p
TAB
p
54
f
rall.
p
a tempo
59
64
p
rall.

Allemande

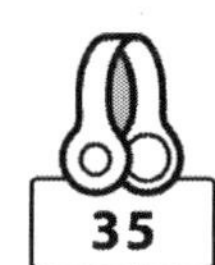

Arranged by
Rob MacKillop

Solo Flute Sonata in Am, BWV 1013

J. S. Bach

Andante

3

5

7

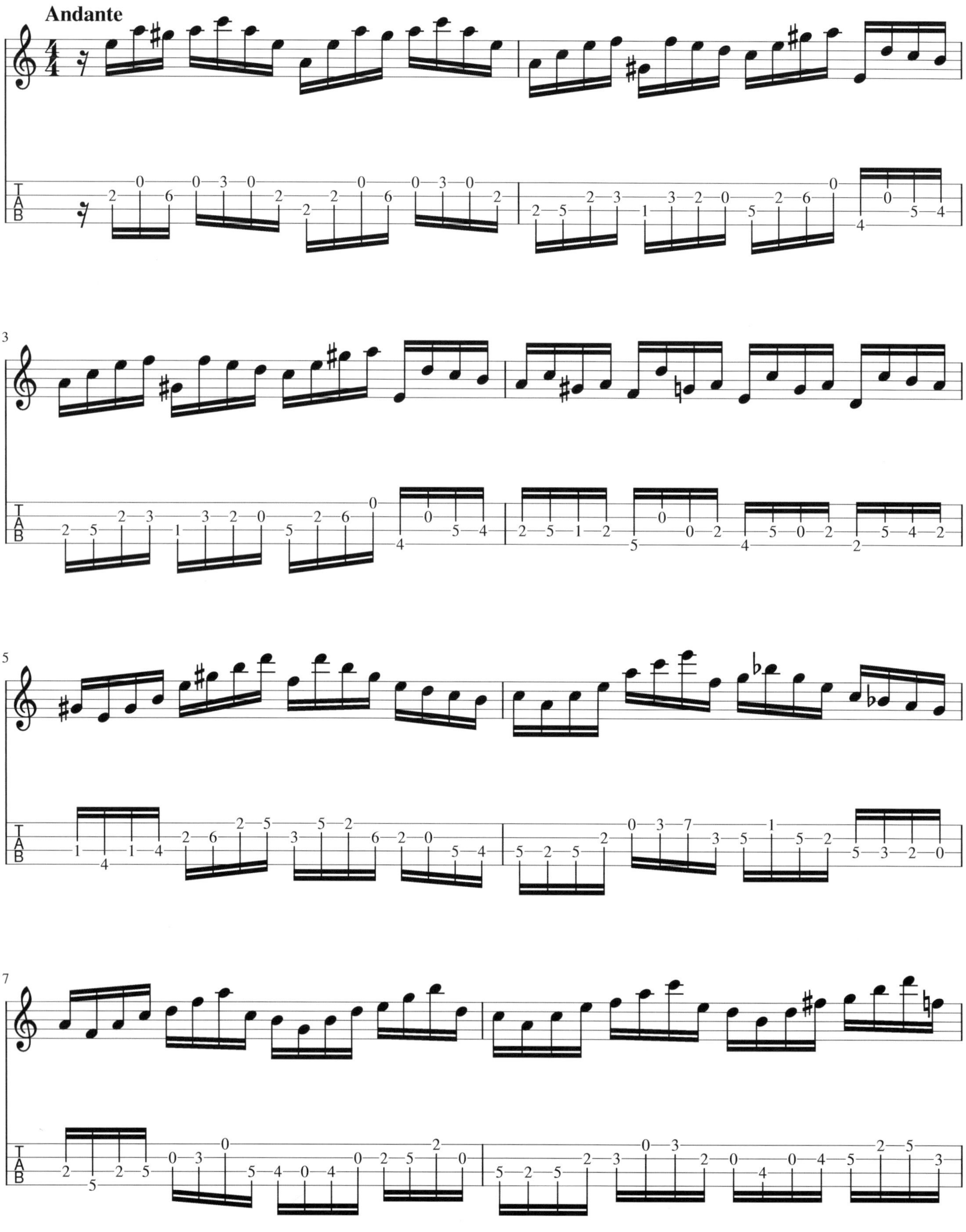

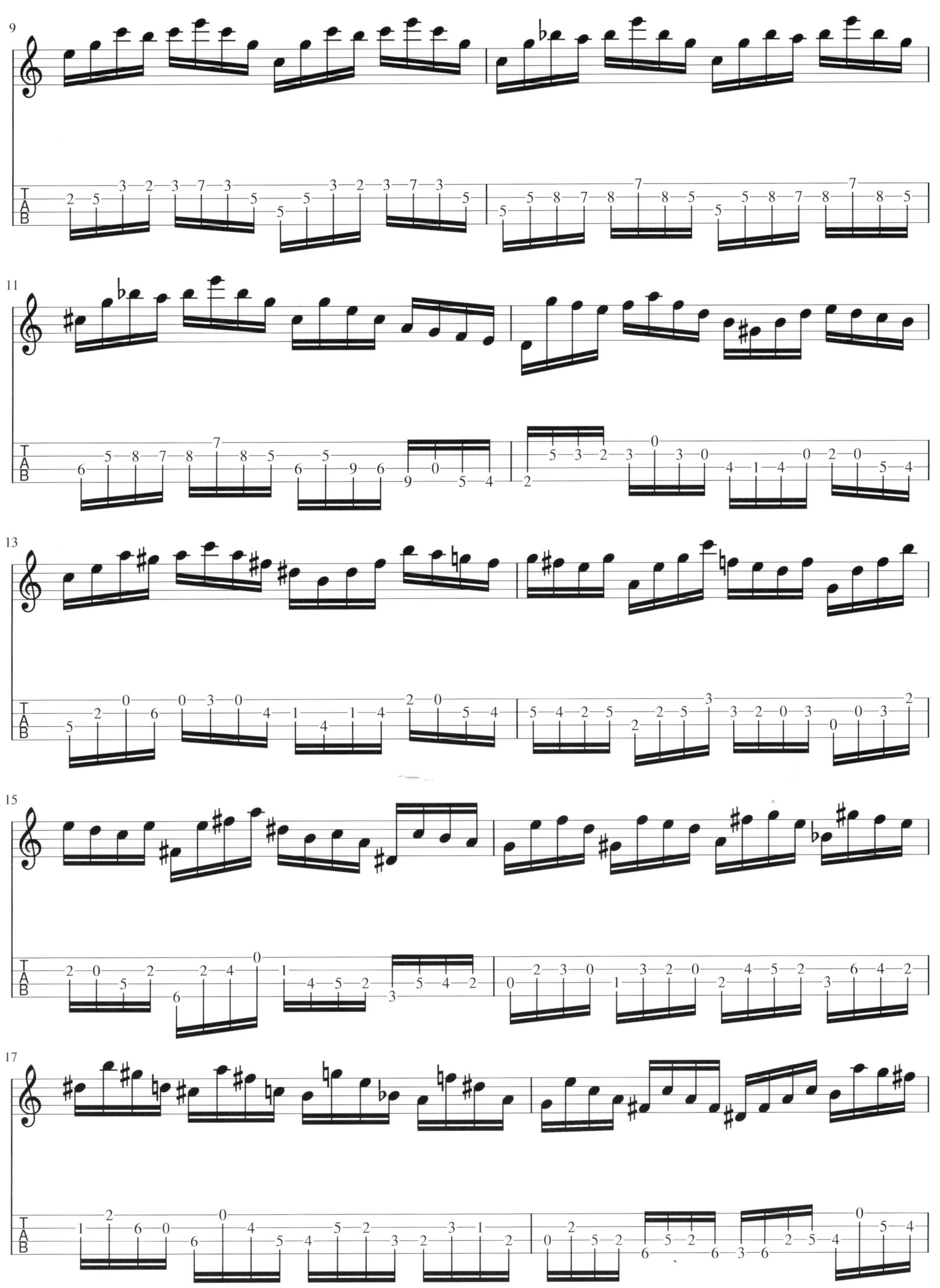
9
11
13
15
17
T
A
B

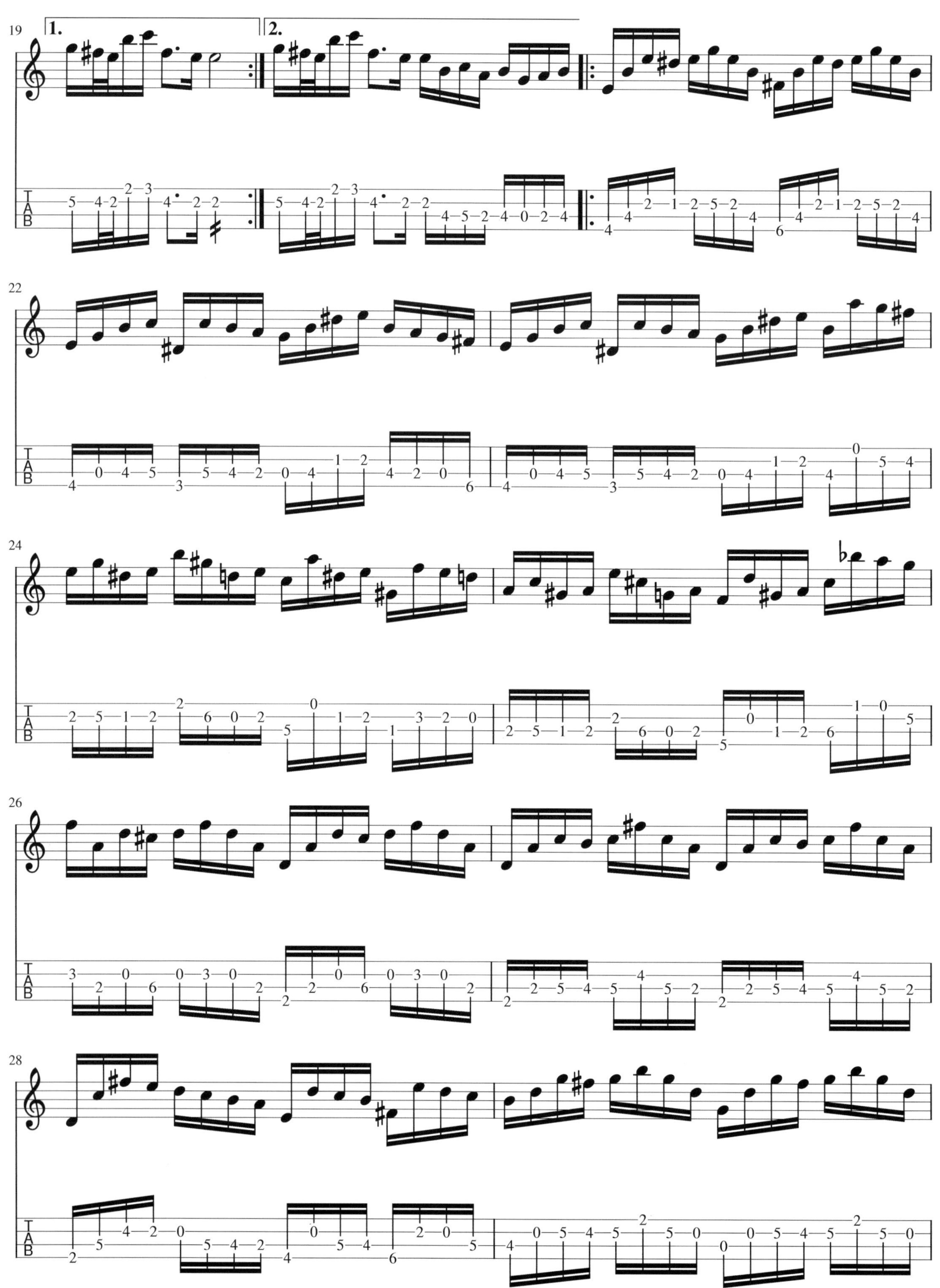
19
1.
2.
TAB
22
24
26
28

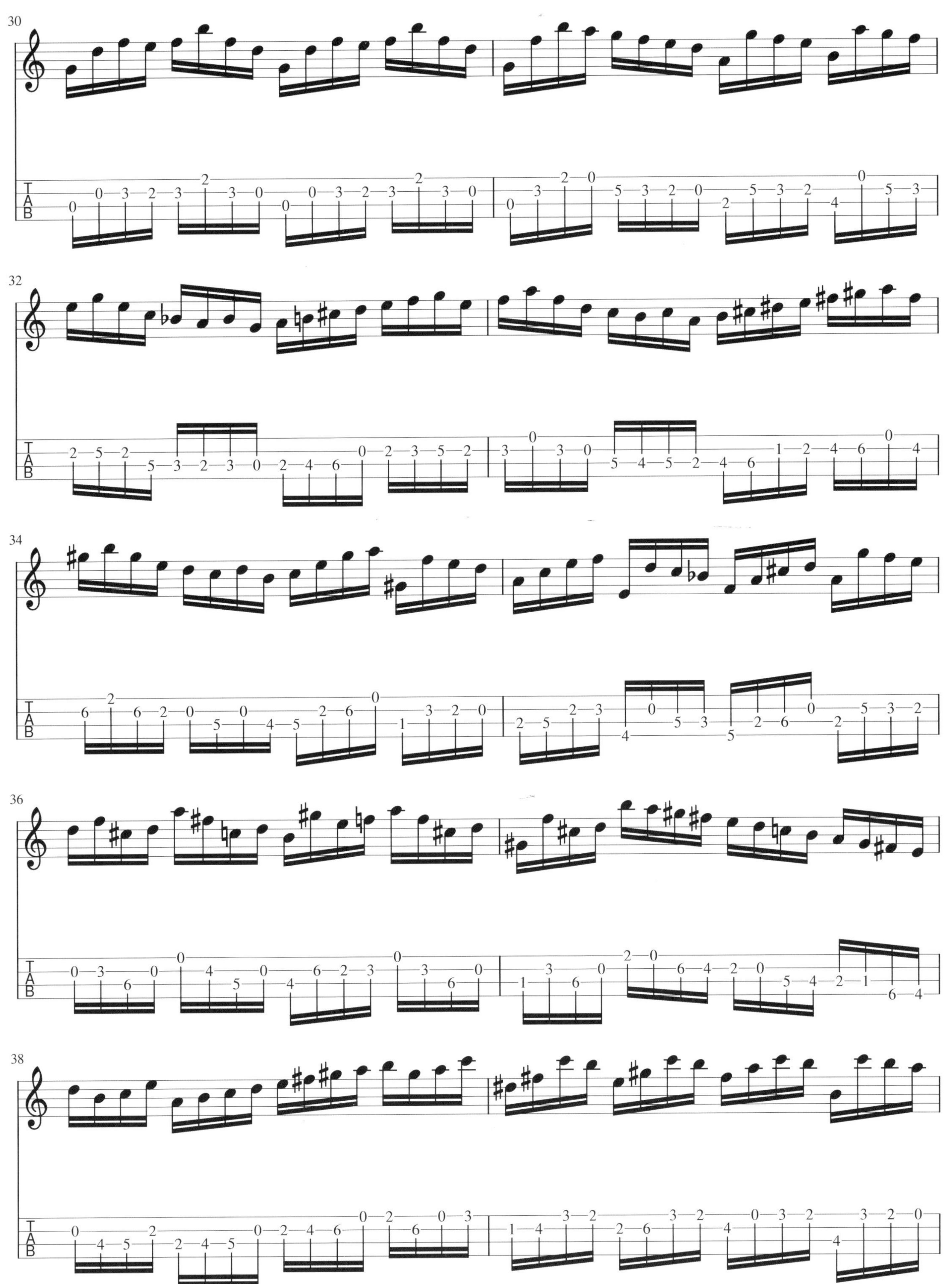
30
TAB
32
TAB
34
TAB
36
TAB
38
TAB

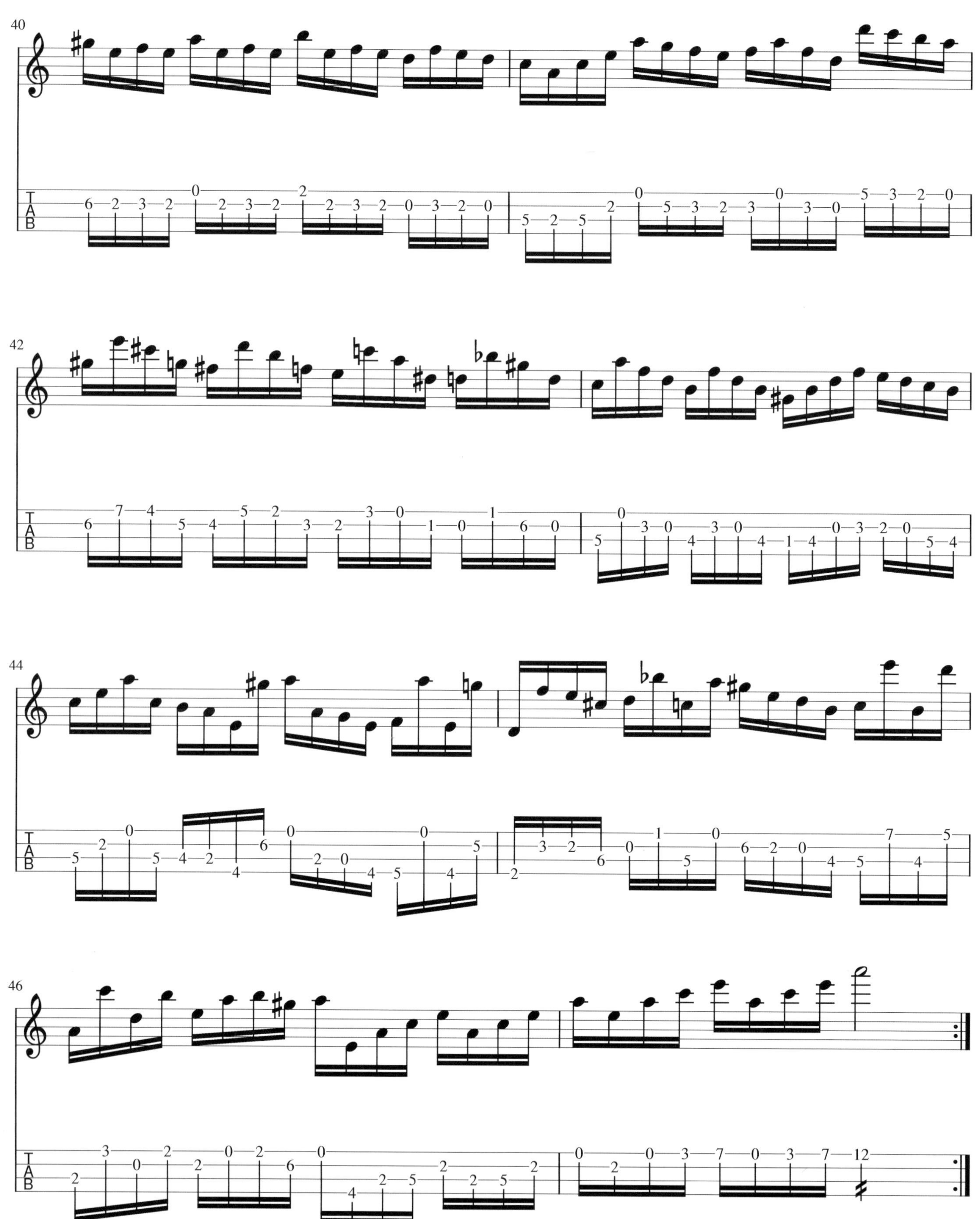
40
T
A
B
42
T
A
B
44
T
A
B
46
T
A
B

This page has been left blank to avoid an awkward page turn.

Arranged by
Rob MacKillop

Courante

Solo Flute Sonata in Am, BWV 1013

J. S. Bach

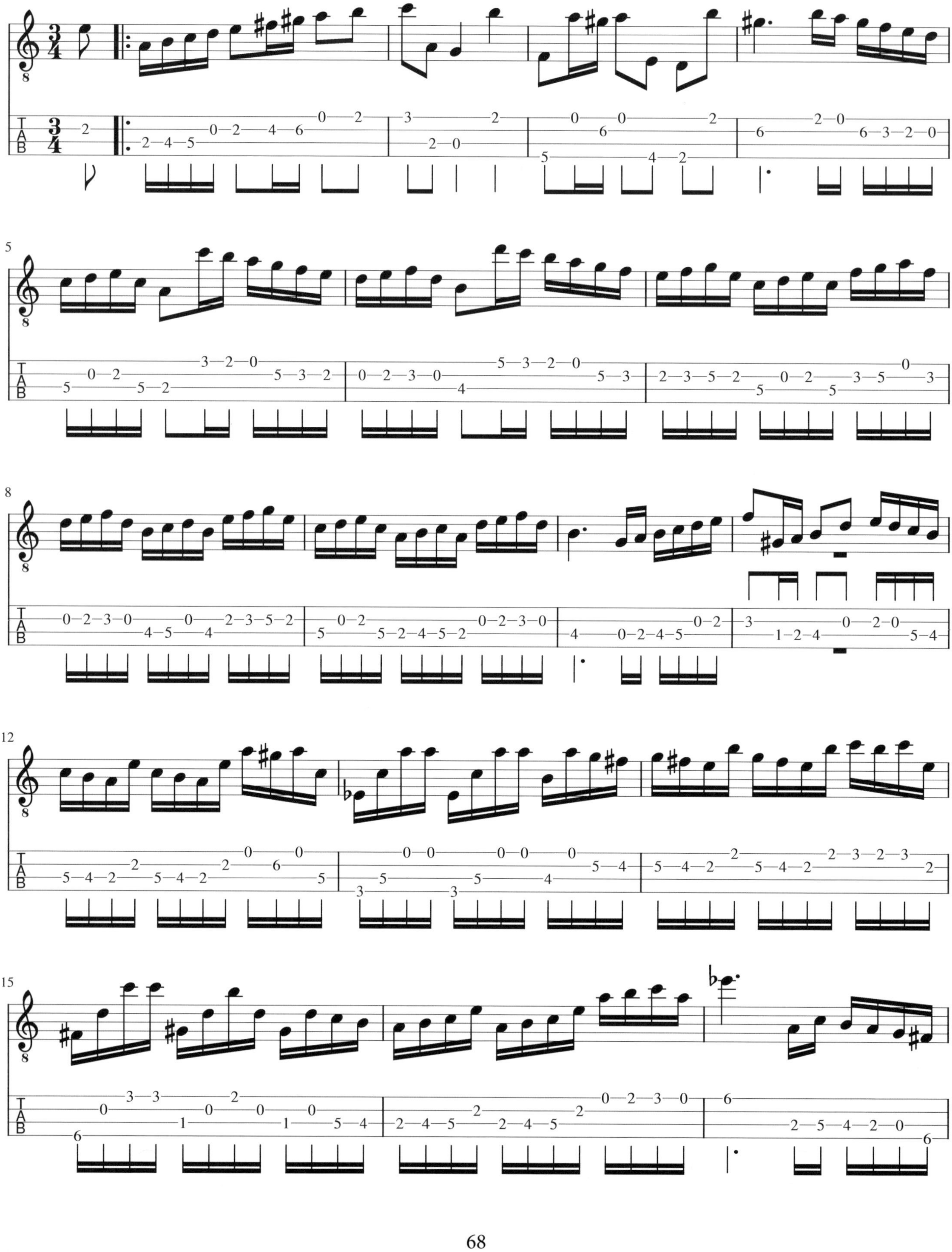

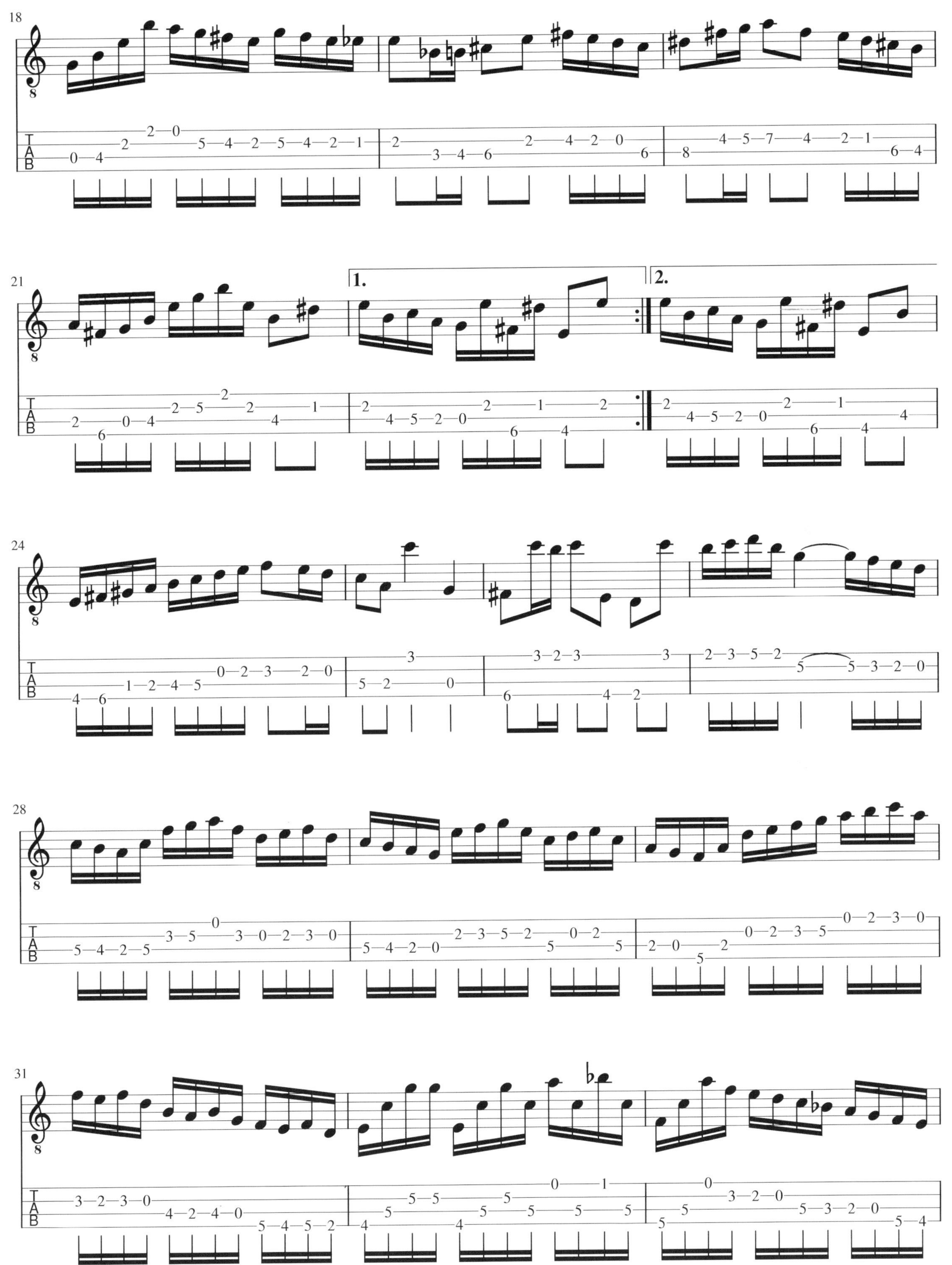

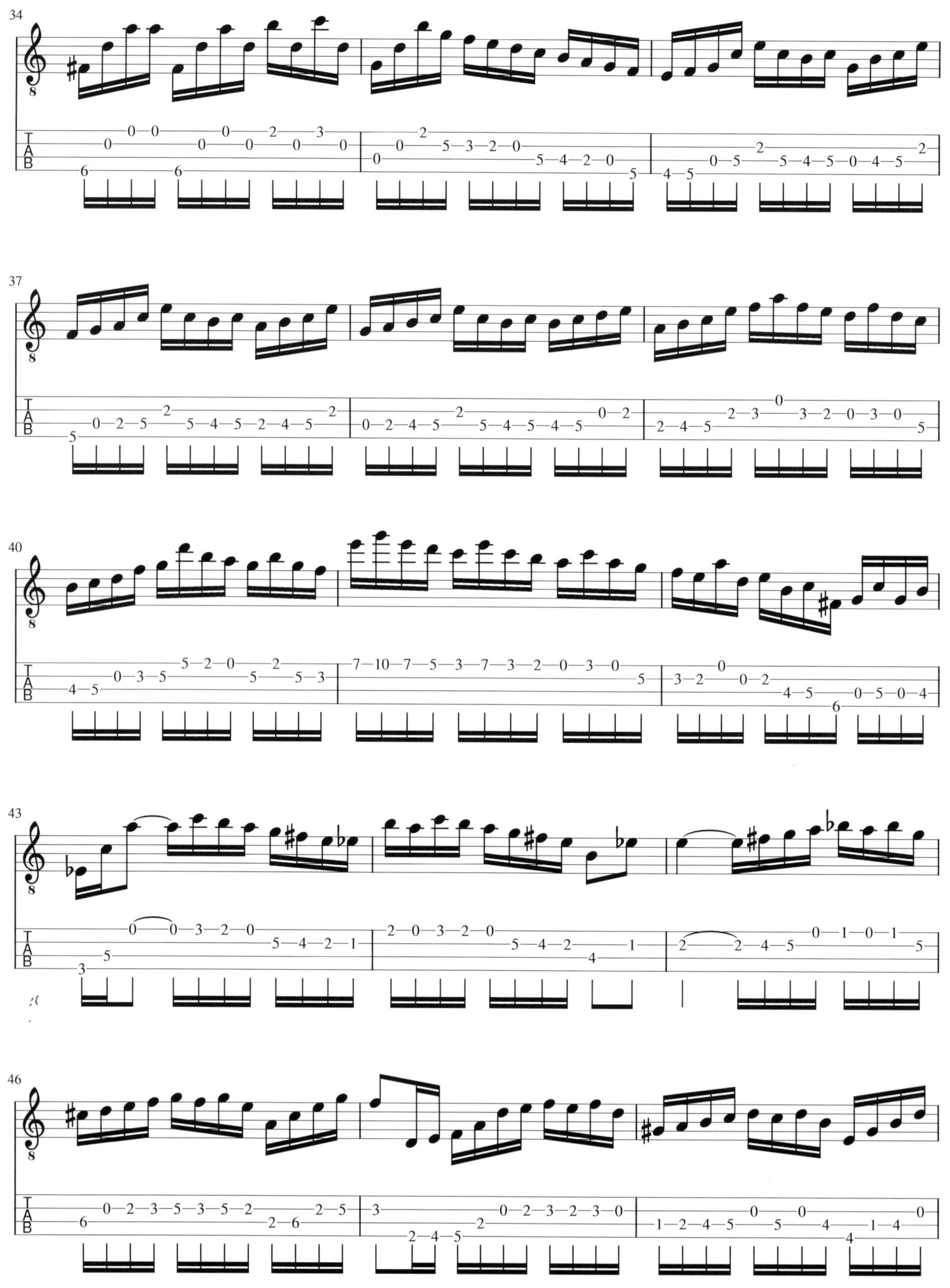
34
37
40
43
46

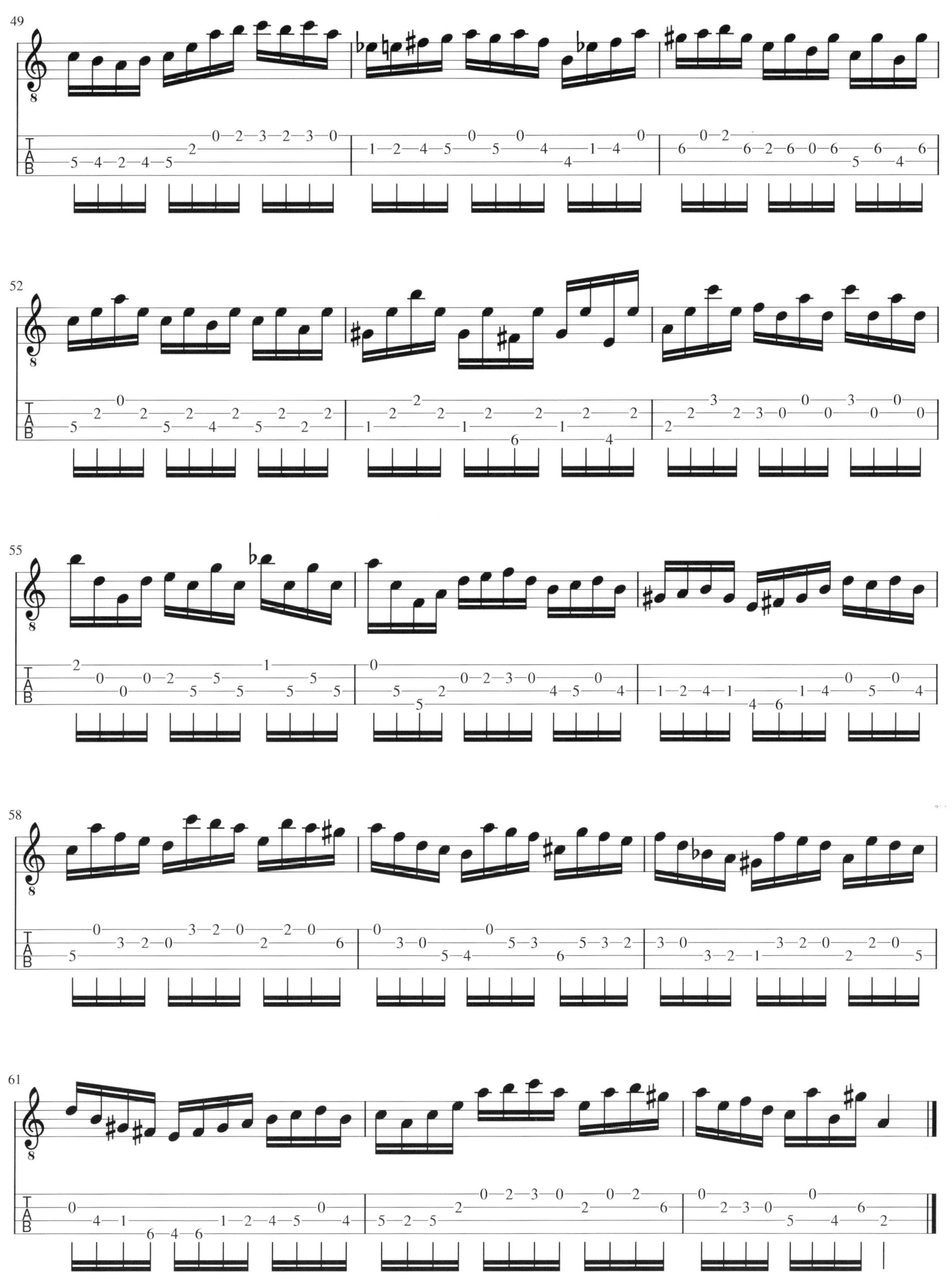
49
52
55
58
61
T
A
B

Sarabande

Arranged by
Rob MacKillop

37

Solo Flute Sonata in Am, BWV 1013

J. S. Bach

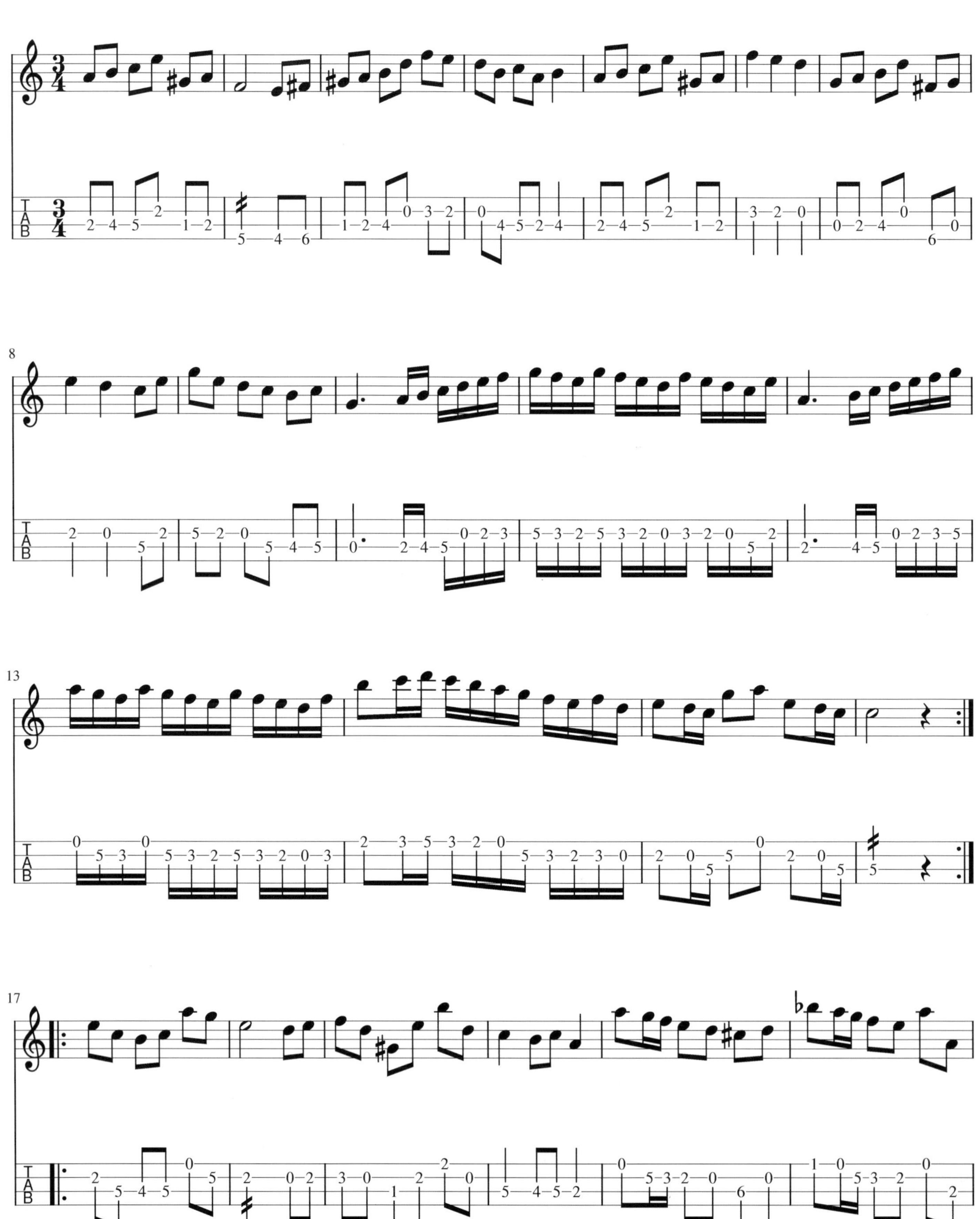

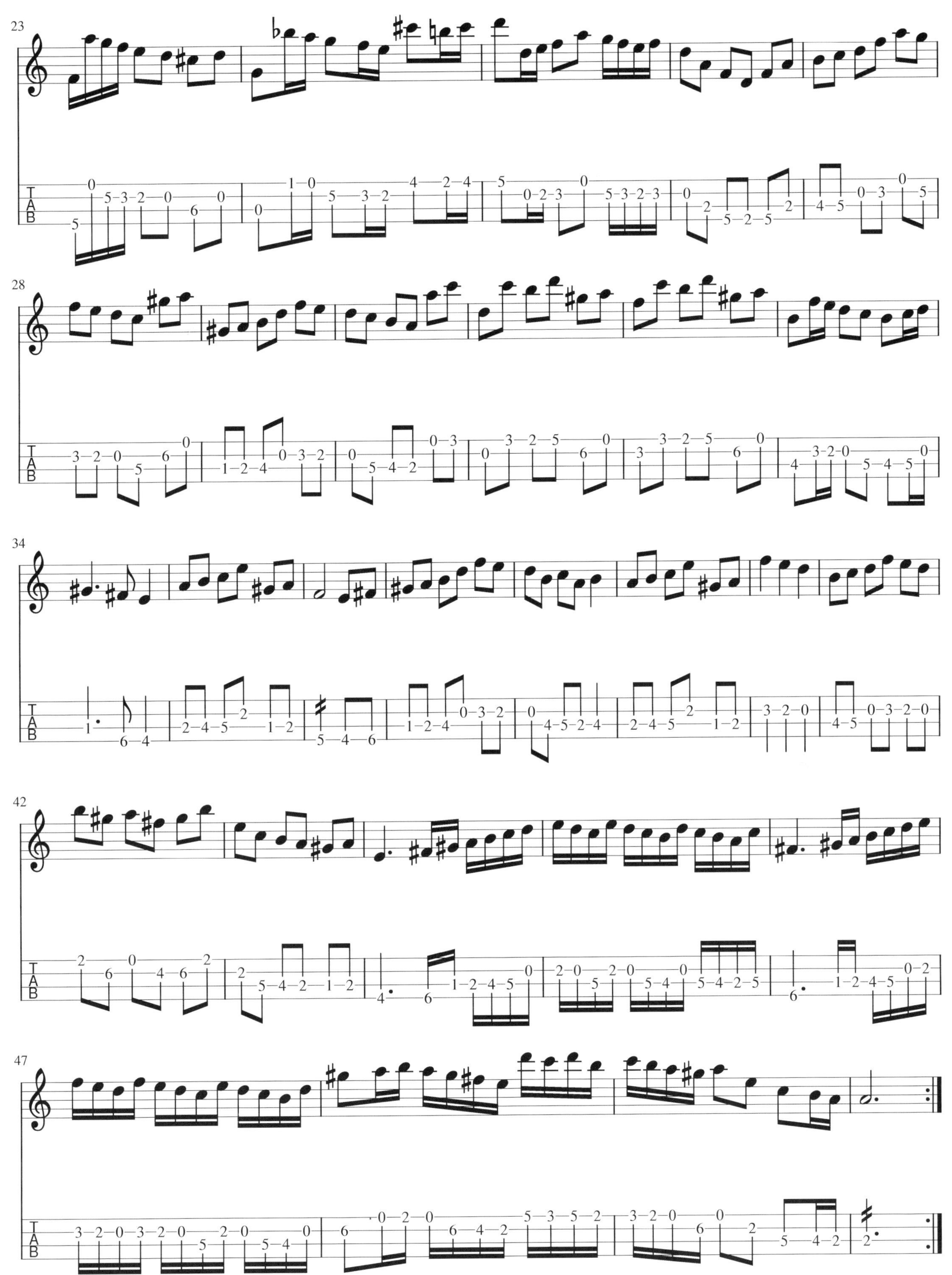

Bourrée Anglaise

Solo Flute Sonata in Am, BWV 1013

Arranged by
Rob MacKillop

J. S. Bach

8

14

1.

22

2.

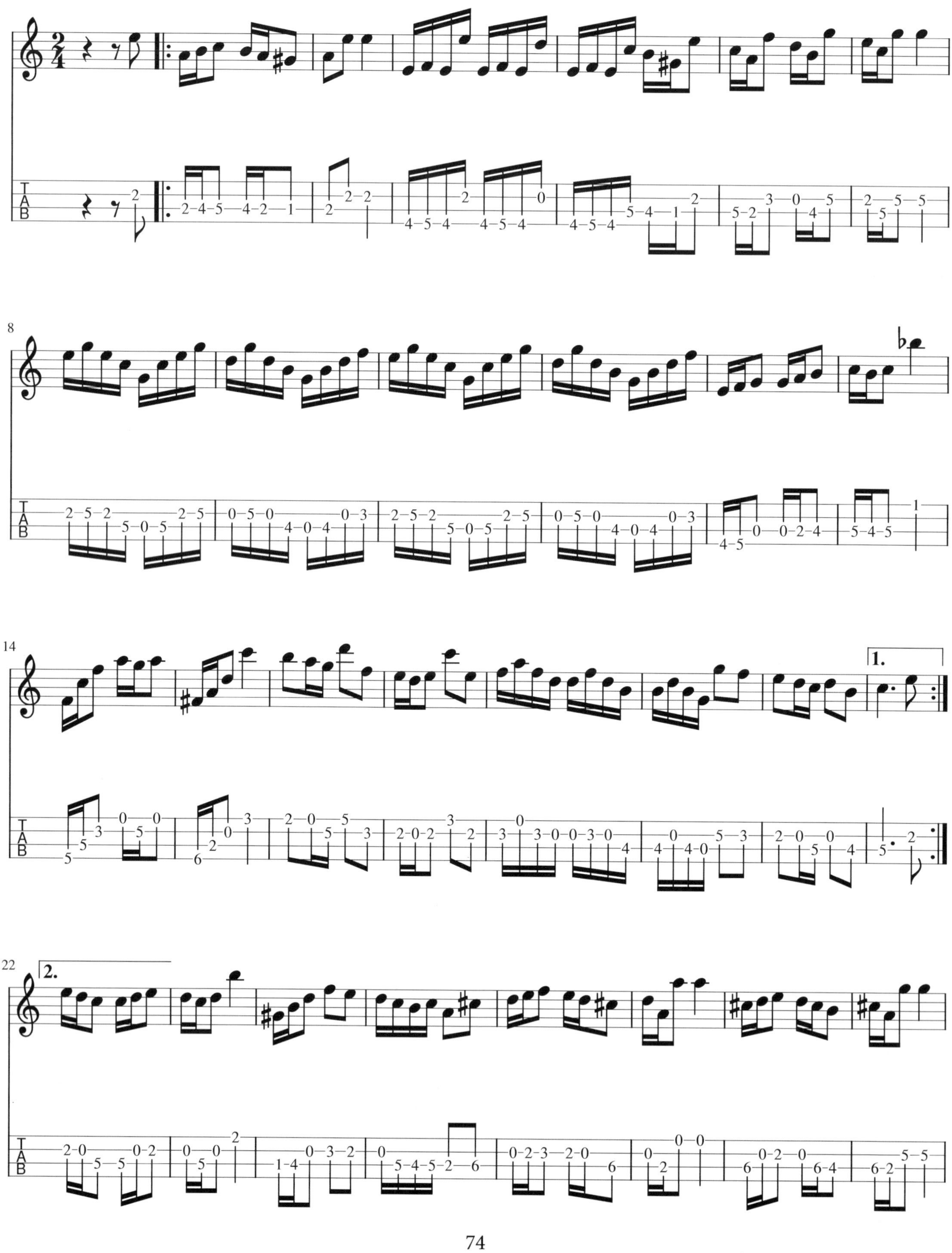

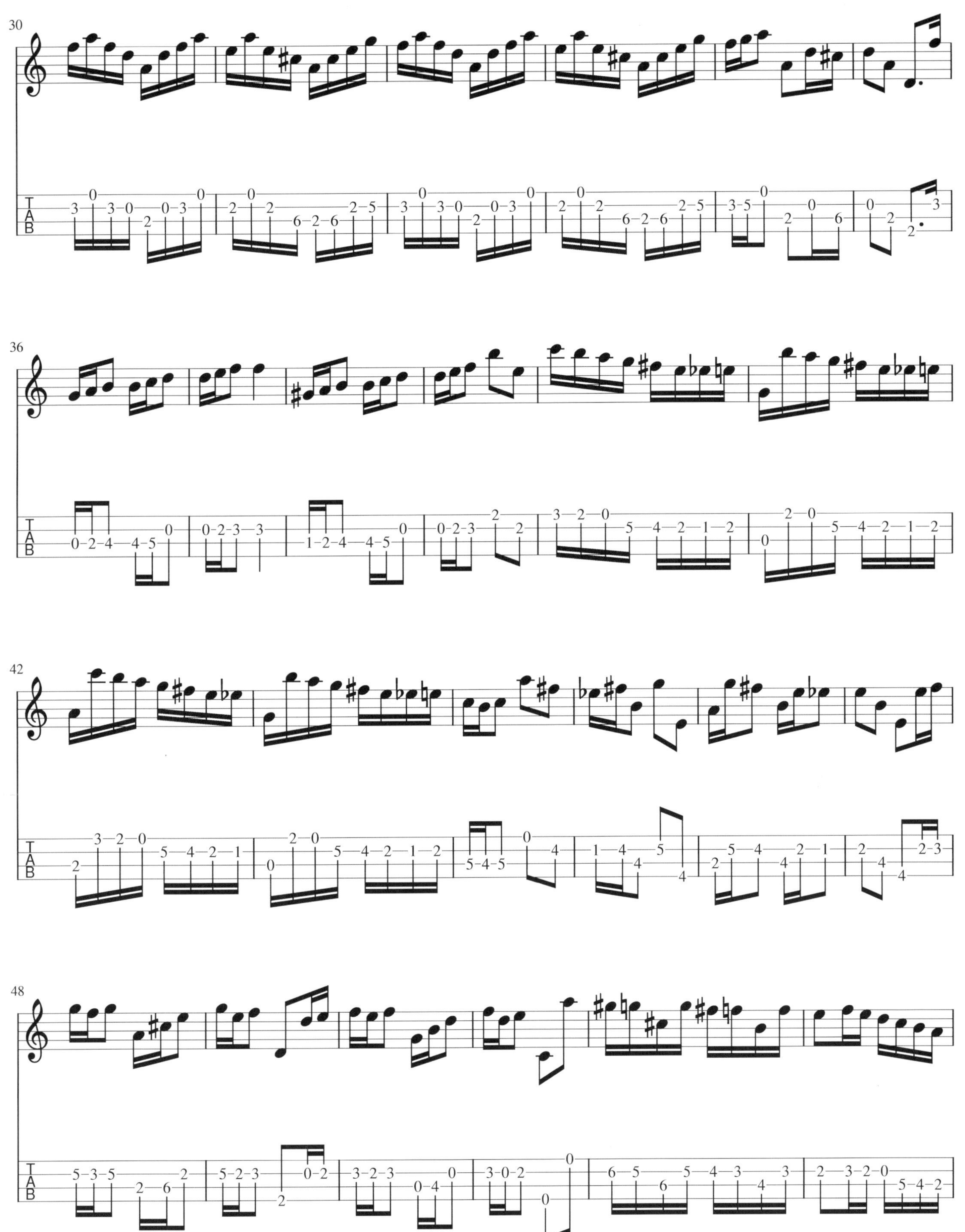

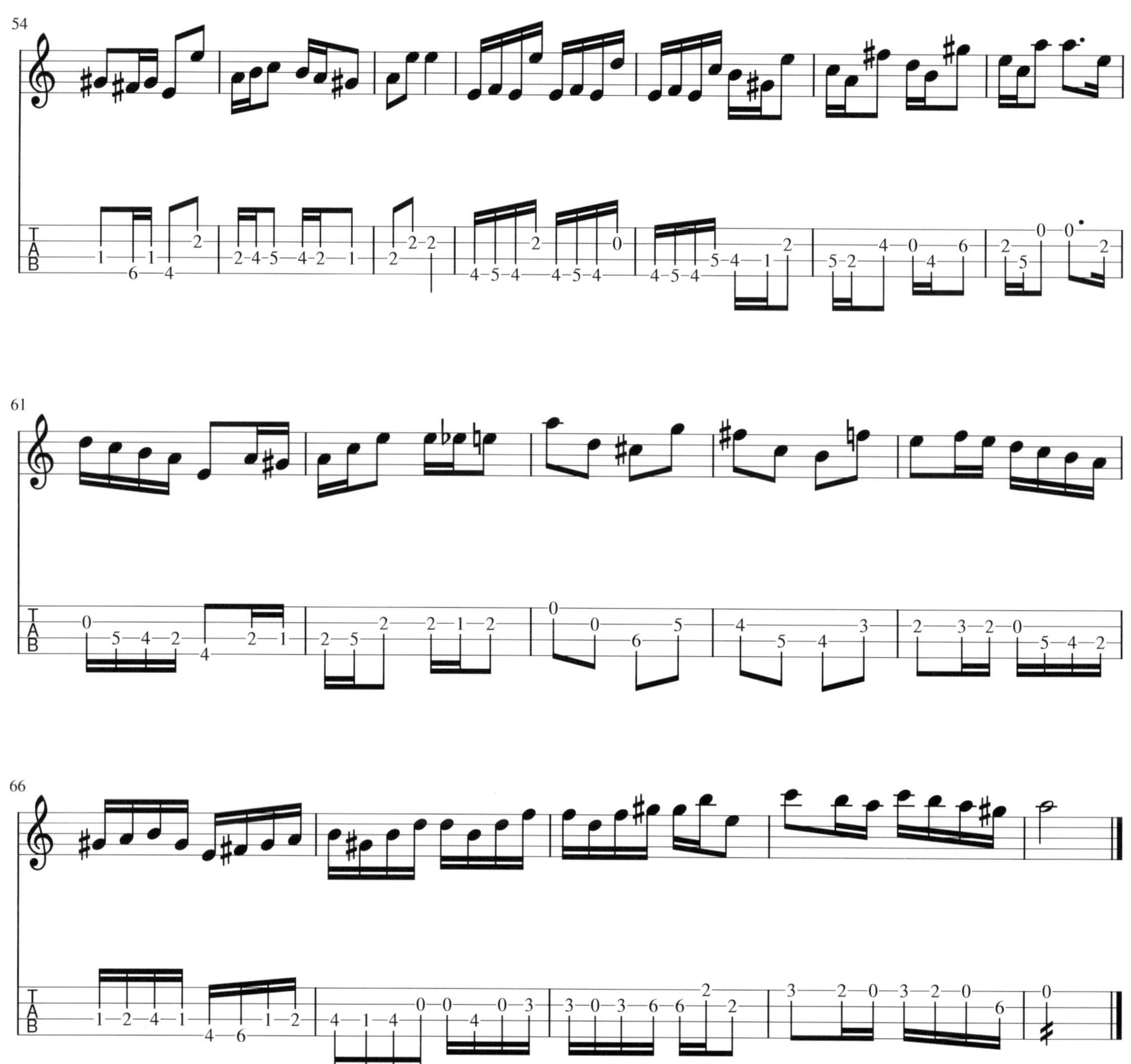
54
TAB
61
TAB
66
TAB

Arranged in
CGDG tuning
by Rob MacKillop

Allemande

Cello Suite No. 5

J. S. Bach

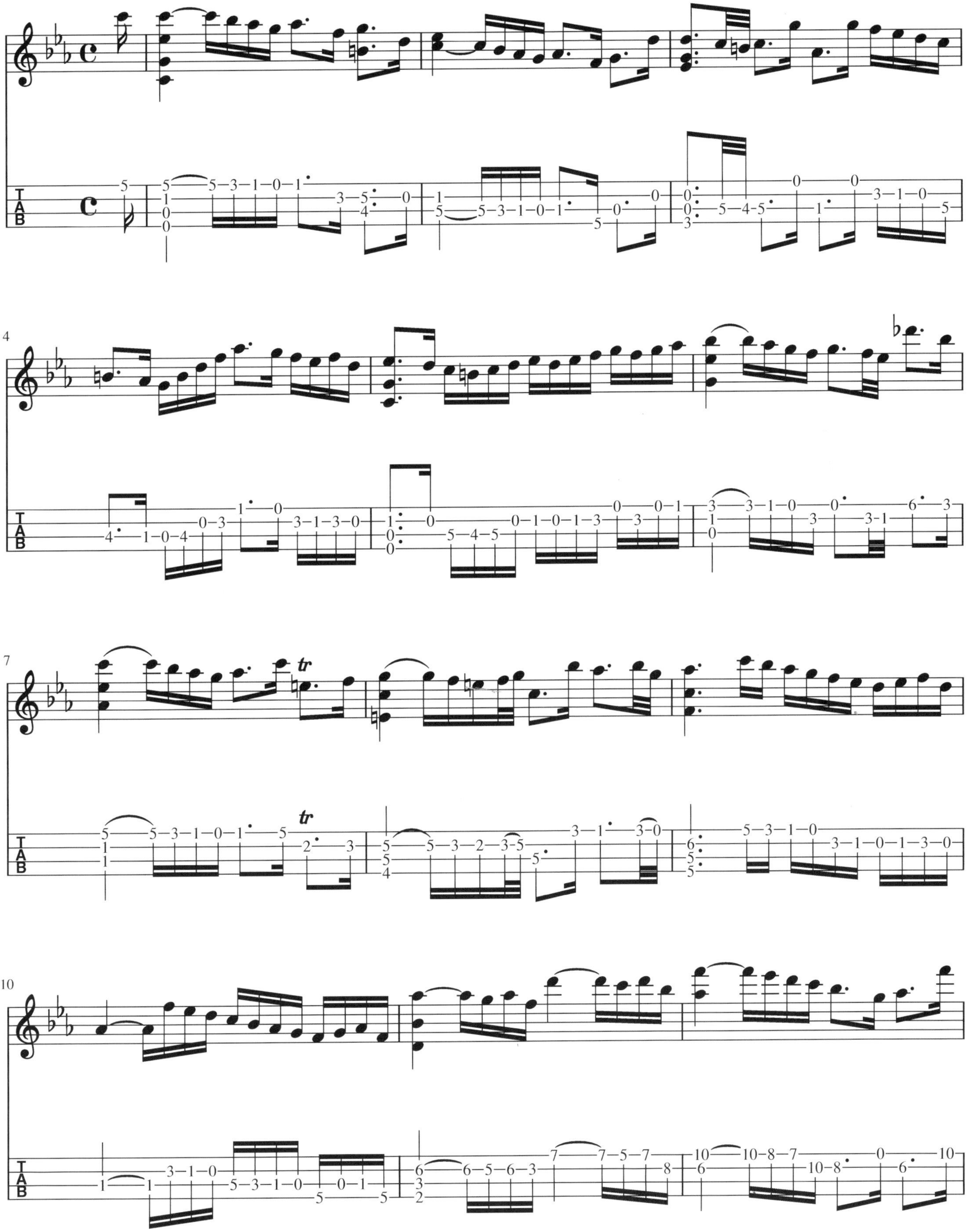

4

7

tr

tr

10

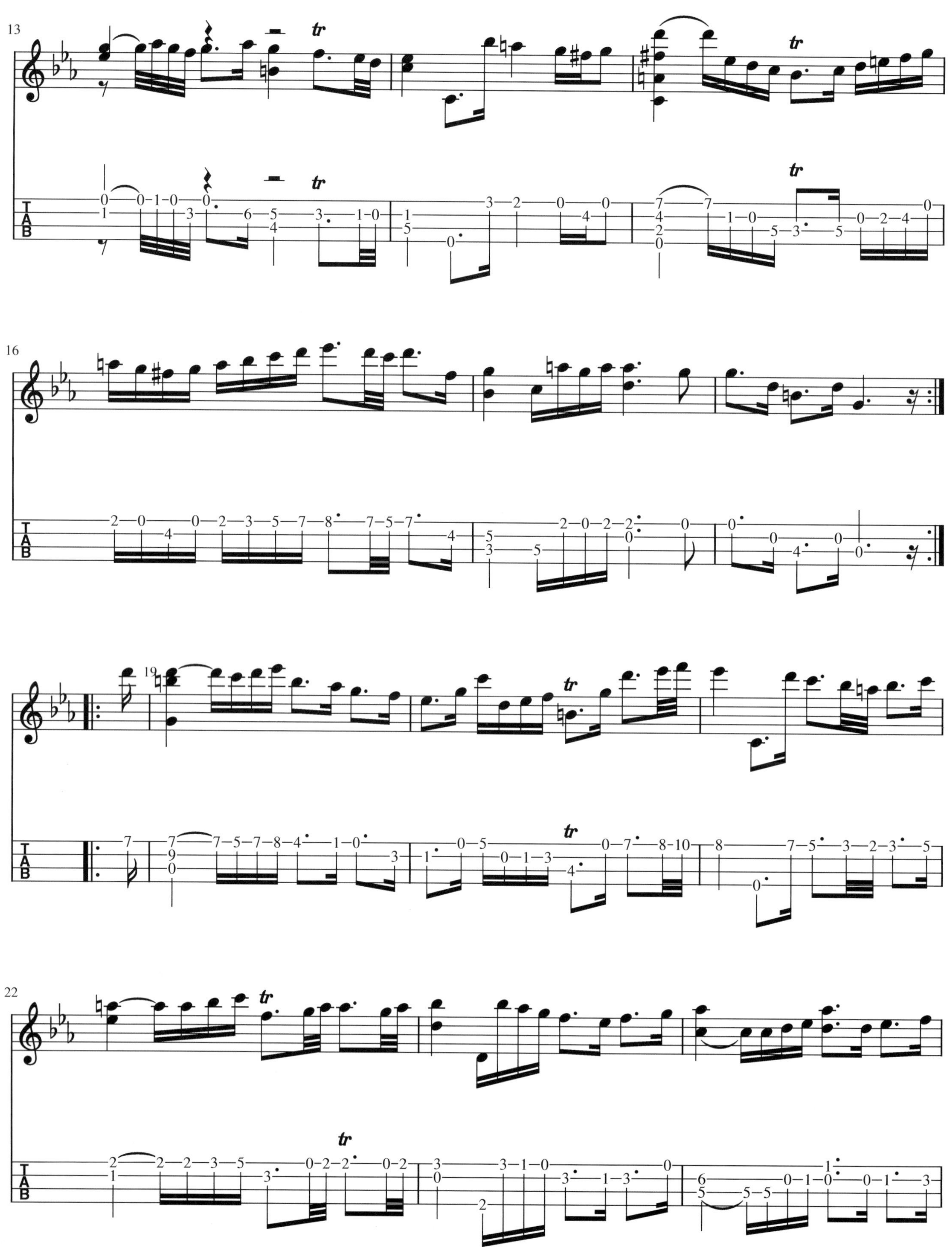
13
tr
TAB
16
TAB
19
tr
TAB
22
tr
TAB

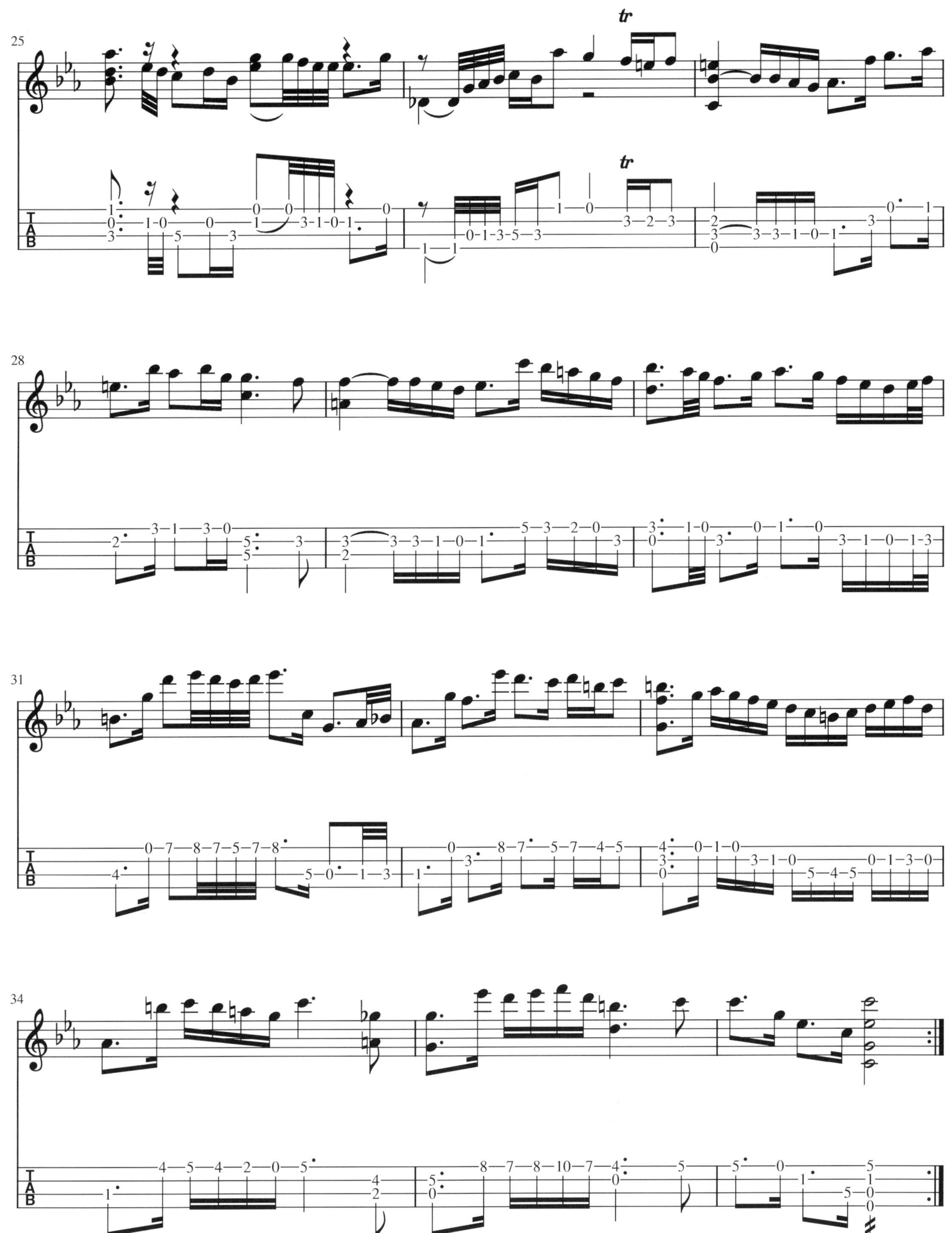
25
tr
tr
T
A
B
28
T
A
B
31
T
A
B
34
T
A
B

Arranged in
CGDG tuning
by Rob MacKillop

40

Sarabande

Cello Suite No.5

J. S. Bach

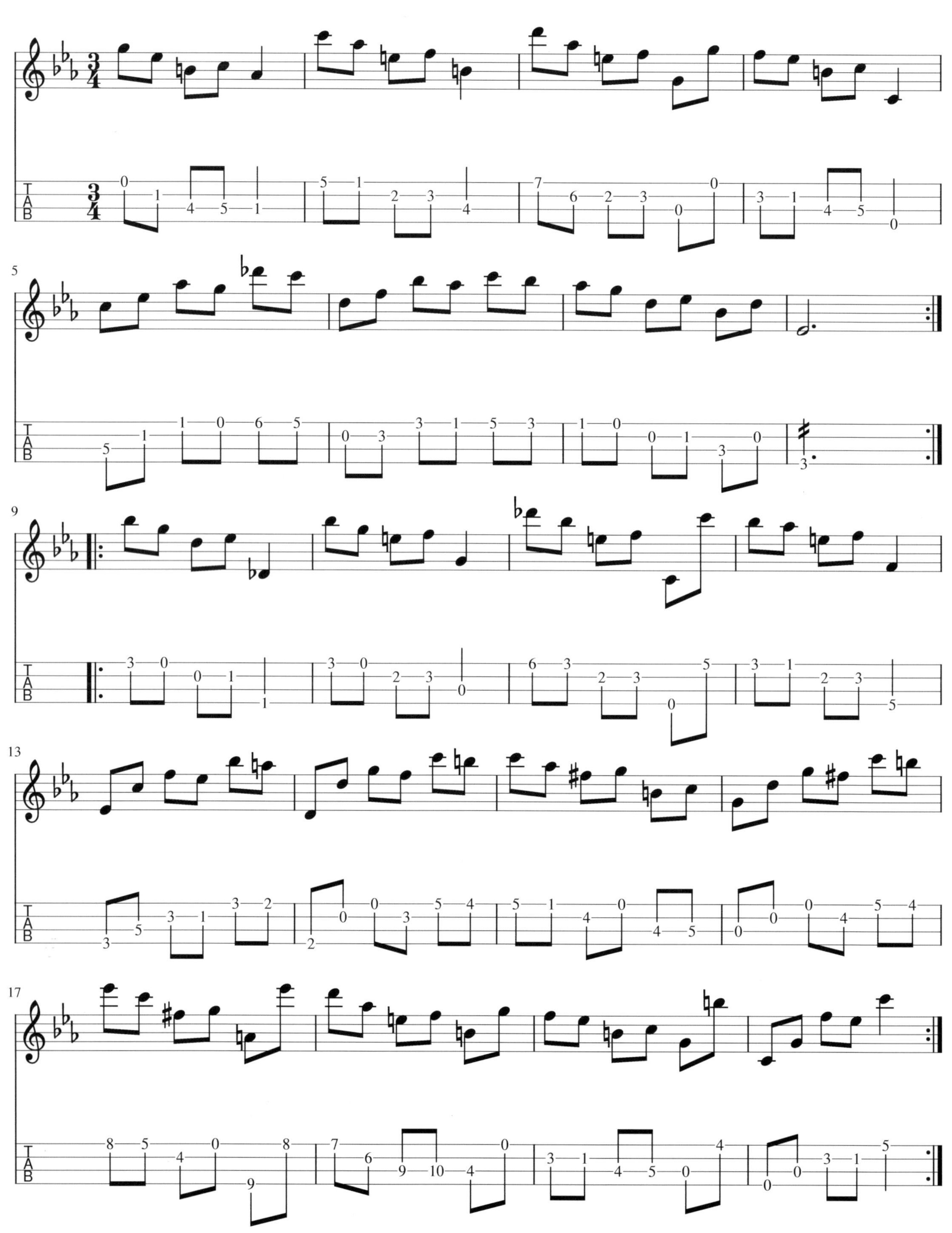